PSYCHE
THE SELFORGANIZING SYSTEM

Three Essays

Peter Zagermann

PSYCHE
THE SELFORGANIZING SYSTEM

Three Essays

IPBOOKS.net
International Psychoanalytic Books

International Psychoanalytic Books (IPBooks)
New York • http://www.IPBooks.net

PSYCHE – The Selforganizing System – Three Essays

Published by IPBooks, Queens, NY
Online at: www.IPBooks.net

ISBN: 978-1-956864-56-4

It's life and life only.

Bob Dylan

Contents

Essay 1 1

  I 1

  Drive and Structure... 1

  II 23

  Beyond the Pleasure Principle 23

  Instincts and their Vicissitudes.................................... 28

  The Ego and the Id 35

  The Oedipus Complex 41

  The Female Oedipus Complex 46

  Sublimation.. 49

  Annihilatory Aggression and Primary Envy 52

  Object constancy and the autistic hole 57

  The Pathologies 66

  Projective Identification 76

  Summary.. 80

Essay 2 On the Metapsychology of the Earliest Mental State 85

Essay 3 Three Theses 121

  I. Mark Solms 121

  II. The Object as Representation of the Life Drive 134

  III. Anorexia and Bulimia as Autistic Breakdown 137

Bibliography.. 141

Essay 1

I

Drive and Structure

If we examine the foundational development of psychoanalytic theory, Freud's pivotal discovery was the existence of the unconscious, followed by the realization that this unconscious possesses a structure and adheres to functional principles. He detailed the oedipal constellation, delineated the three phases of psychosexual development, and proposed a dualistic drive conception that forms the basis of the psychic organism in terms of energy and content.

Melanie Klein extended this by discovering early forms of object relation through the splitting of the object in the infantile paranoid-schizoid and depressive positions. She regarded the good-bad split in the infantile paranoid-schizoid position as the primary functional form of the psyche, arising directly from the dichotomy of pleasure and unpleasure or love and hate.

But then Frances Tustin, in 1972 and 1981, described psychogenic primary encapsulation autism, the earliest and most severe form of mental illness. It had not been recognized for a long time that this clinical picture necessitates an extension of the psychoanalytic theory of psychic structure formation, as it cannot be explained based on the splitting concept of object relation. This serves as the starting point for the considerations I present below.

In essence, the task is to demonstrate the outcomes that arise when one begins with the most straightforward basic assumption, which inherently explains itself, and then develops the logical consequences that follow from it. It's crucial to note that my objective is not to establish true or false claims but to develop a theory as a model, proving its value through internal consistency and its ability to incorporate the existing clinically validated theoretical fragments of psychoanalysis, along with integrating new clinical findings.

Naturally, my thoughts have connections and resonances in all directions of the existing psychoanalytic literature. I've chosen not to delve into these cross-references, focusing instead on explaining the advocated model as clearly as possible. This is because the model is complex on its own, and there are no direct dependencies on other considerations.

To clarify, when I refer to independence, I do not mean this in the sense of arrogant detachment from the "rest" of psychoanalytic research but rather in demonstrating the conclusions derived from the purely logical development of a simplest, axiomatic primary hypothesis. Independence here implies a reliance on the logical development of the line of thought, not a devaluation of other considerations. Conformity with other considerations and findings serves as confirmation but does not serve as causal justification.

The basic idea, from which the structure formation of the psyche as well as its pathological deviations can be broken down in this sense in a discipline-specific logical step-by-step argumentation, is that at the moment when the first sensory perceptions become possible due to the ontogenetic maturation of the central nervous system, these perceptions by definition have a bipolar structure. They consist of the pole of the perceiving subject and the pole of the perceived itself, that is, of the representation. Here, when I refer to perception in a fundamental sense, I mean the ability to construct the central representation of an afferent stimulus. In this context, the first neuronal representation coincides with the first psychoanalytic representation. I propose the operative hypothesis that, in psychoanalytic terms, the perceiving subject is immediately the archaic, primordial ego, while the perceived – that is, the representation – is the archaic, primordial object.

This initiates the dimension of the psychical, suggesting that the ego, not the id, should be considered the first instance of the psychic apparatus.

By operative hypothesis I mean that this assumption can only be retrogradely justified by the clinical plausibility of the consequences derived from it.

From the derivation of this new dimension from perception, it follows that the psychical is bound to the separateness and juxtaposition of ego and object representation, since this follows from the structure of the act of perception. It represents a constitutive non-identity of ego and object, implying *that any psychic movement that attacks this separateness of ego and object endangers the dimension of the psychical itself.* This conclusion has significant implications in terms of a generally valid clinical maxim.

Perception has a neurological substrate in neuronal representation, but as *psychic* process of perception of the primary object by the primary ego, it is a phantasmatic act conditioned and enabled by the system properties of the cerebral cortex that constitute human perception. This phantasmatic act is annulled by the fusing of subject and object of perception, resulting in the annulment of the dimension of the psychical arising from perception.

With the addition of physiological need pressure, such a simple system inevitably encounters a conflict, establishing the conflictual nature of human psychic life. The primary ego, under the pressure of need, attempts to incorporate the primary sensory object into its own identity, carrying out a fusional movement. In this world consisting only of the early ego and the primary object, the abolition of unpleasure – the sensation of deficiency in the realm of the ego – is localized in the object, since there is no other outside of the ego than that of this primary object, and the abolition of deficiency in the ego evidently must come from the outside.

This fusional movement is the beginning of psychic activity in the sense of an archaic, *sensorially determined wish*. It leads to a constitutive conflict, as the intended fusion of the ego with the object would collapse the bipolar world of inner perception, which has just unfolded in the opposition of perceiving ego and perceived object and out of which the dimension of the psychical is to develop. This – inevitable – fusional movement is, in my definition, the – thus purely psychically defined – death drive, as it would abolish perception and, consequently, the psyche itself. The ontic force opposing it, aiming to maintain and secure the emerging dimension of the psychical, is the life drive. Its goal is to keep the ego and the representation of the object separate. Its instrument is the fear of ego dissolution that would result from a fusional realization. Since the preservation of the object in the face of its dissolution in the fusional movement is the interest of the life drive, the life drive is *the objectifying force in the psyche*. Both drives are, therefore, psychic productions in this understanding.

It is crucial to understand the properties of the primary object from different aspects: Firstly, this primordial, sensory-based object does not yet have anything to do with a human other. It is the precipitation of unassigned coenesthetic stimuli, originating from the external world as well as being of proprioceptive, enteroceptive or central nervous provenance, held together solely by their temporal contiguity. No distinction can yet be made between an inside and an outside of the body or person, and a concept of reality does not yet exist. It is about the level of the very first object representations in the sense of the precipitation of the sensory stimulations organized – that is consolidated – only by simultaneity within a primordial constitution, which does not yet know any differentiated mental contents, i.e. phantasies, thoughts or symbols, apart from the sensory stimulation, because the mental space necessary for this has not yet been built up. These archaic objects of sensory perception bear a striking resemblance to those inanimate two-dimensional object formations that we know from the early and severe autistic disorders. As we all start out with perception, it has to be assumed that we have all passed through this archaic state of object constitution. Notably, the animation of the object in the process of primary identification has not yet taken place.

From my perspective, this might be the reason why Margaret Mahler arrived at her incorrect understanding of a primary autistic phase. As sufficiently discussed, such a phase does not exist in terms of the specific psychodynamics of the primary autistic condition as detailed by Frances Tustin. This psychodynamics were not yet clarified and described at the time of Mahler's formulations. However, what does exist is the level of primitive object constitution common to all human beings, to which the primary autists have remained fixated. This level is characterized by an entirely internal, intrapsychic genesis of the object representation, hence the "autistic" misunderstanding.

Inasmuch as stimulations from all possible sensory sources converge upon this primary object, and these stimulations are interconnected solely by their temporal contiguity, this primary object incorporates stimuli originating both from the subject's sphere and the general environment, *particularly from the surrounding maternal organism*. Notably, according to established findings, we find ourselves still within the intrauterine situation regarding the origins of perceptual function and, according to my hypothesis, the genesis of psychic experience. These amalgamated, baked-together object constructions, encountered, for instance, in the treatment of autistic children or severe regressions, convey the semblance of a symbiotic form of experience.

It is crucial to underscore that, from a metapsychological standpoint, this perspective is misleading. The primary object is the primary object – in terms of what is perceived – irrespective of the origin of its sensory elements. *The primary experience is not symbiotic* in the sense of a fundamental indistinctness between ego and object representation. This misconception gives rise to a theoretically consequential error, as clinical data misinterpreted in this way have led to the presumption of a primordial symbiotic chaos where somatic stimuli, self and object representations are in an undistinguished confusion. Descriptively accurate, yes, but this is precisely the primary object.

The theoretical framework adopted has a profound influence on the approach to clinical situations, as the analytic attitude can significantly differ based on the underlying assumptions about the psyche's primary structural constitution. Assuming a factual symbiotic fusion as this foundation diverges markedly from understanding that a symbiotic representation possesses object character. If one assumes the former, the analytical work might erroneously focus on disentangling this presumed innate symbiotic fusion between the self and the other, while the objectal interpretation acknowledges that the seeming fusional chaos is a very normal step within development, i.e. without psychopathological significance.

6

On its corresponding level of the structurally simplest organization of mental constitution, the primary object is the only thing that exists. An outside beyond the primary object is not yet conceivable, as such an outside, as I will elucidate shortly, presupposes the experience of time as the correlate of an incipient object constancy. However, I define object constancy differently than the usage in ego psychology, namely as the mental persistence – or constancy – of a representation beyond the temporal scope of the immediate stimulus situation it depicts.

The mental concept of time, of temporal progression, emerges from the evolving overview of a series of momentary stimulus states – the initial rudiments of formation of experience. These momentary stimulus states constitute the respective evocations of the primary object. Hence, the formation of experience, which necessitates the persistence of the representation of the primary object beyond the moment of the actual stimulus situation, is synonymous with the commencement of object constancy. Only through object constancy can an object representation be compared with a preceding one, i.e. the comparison of experiences, initially manifesting as a temporal comparison, as within a mental constitution not yet conditioned, the present stimulus constellation is represented as a global representation filling the entirety of the given moment of time, depicting the respective activated primary object. From this temporal comparison arises the concept of the outside of the object, concurrent with that of its boundary, limitation, and thus relativity.

To articulate this point differently for clarity: As long as the primary object of time moment A, due to the as yet undeveloped rudimentary constancy, cannot be compared with the primary object of time moment B, firstly, objects A and B cannot be contextualized with each other, and secondly, there is no external dimension to the primary object. This mental concept of the outside presupposes time and the comparative evaluation of objects within that temporal framework. For the primary ego, therefore, the primary object, in this primordial condition prior to the establishment of representational object constancy, is, so to speak, *the universe, the all-that-is, beyond which nothing exists*. Its characteristics are totality and globality.

This also implies that the primary object in this phase, before the establishment of object constancy, cannot yet be split. The good-bad split of the object necessitates the mental maintenance of the counter-image of the split representation in the psychic background as a definitional requirement. Object splitting, therefore, requires object constancy. We find ourselves in a realm of psychic experience antecedent to the mechanisms and experiential qualities of the paranoid-schizoid position, constituting a *pre-schizoid phase.*

By extension, these lines of reasoning should be applied to the ego itself. The ego, as the subject of perception, appears, from a perspective related to subjective experience, just at the most elementary level of its function in every individual moment in time, in its full potential identity and energetic wholeness. Even though it might appear deficient and fragmented when observed externally, the primary ego lacks reflective distance from itself. There is no relativization of the ego through the comparison of its states in time, just as there is no concept of an external dimension to the object and thus no relativization of the object. In essence, the criteria of totality and globality not only apply to the primary object but equally to the primary ego.

Significantly, this consideration has direct implications for the viewpoint that regards the infantile notion of omnipotence as a defensive formation against the experience of primary helplessness. Viewing this as an adultomorphism, the early infantile experience lacks the ability to recognize its objective helplessness, requiring access to reality, which is not present in this primordial state. The situation is quite the opposite: infantile omnipotence is primary, bestowed with tremendous force, and stems from the absence of obligation to any real condition.

In any case, if ego and object, in the original act and event of perception, constitute themselves in the same moment ex nihilo and if their relationship with each other is that of perceiving subject and the perceived, this signifies on the energetic plane that the ego's primary and spontaneous cathexis of the object is the inaugural event with which psychic life begins, the immediate given. Therefore, there is no primary cathexis of the ego alone, as suggested by Freud's pseudopodia model, and the object is not invested by the withdrawal of cathexes from the ego. The concept of an original energetic wholeness, completeness, and unity of the ego, conditioned or constrained by the libido drain to invest the object, is untenable. Thus, I not only assert the existence of a pre-schizoid phase but also challenge the assumption of a phase or state of primary narcissism.

To summarize: In this pre-schizoid phase, the ego *and* the object hold absolute importance; it is characterized by the constitutive criterion of timelessness, and the primary object cannot undergo a split since a splitting alternative cannot be conceived due to the undeveloped object constancy as the capacity to compare representations in time. Splitting needs the capacity of keeping representations constant in time. The onset of the infantile paranoid-schizoid position is presumed to occur with the acquisition of object constancy.

If these assertions about the primary functioning of the mental apparatus hold true, it logically follows that there can be no representation of an experience of unpleasure, of unlust as a bad, rejecting and refusing object in this primary constitution. If an experience of unpleasure were to translate into the representation of a bad object, the ego at this functional level, where the primary object is the All, outside of which nothing exists, would be confronted with a bad cosmos. *This is inconceivable, as the ego would then have to deny its only available object, tantamount to self-deprivation of the basis of life.*

An even more essential argument leading to the same result is the following: According to our primary hypothesis, the initial situation is that the primary ego, in dealing with an experience of deficiency, can see the means of remedying this deficiency only in the primary object. The ego, therefore, in fusion with the primary object, attempts to appropriate this means of remedying the deficiency, the lack.

However, if the primary object is indeed the means of rectifying, of remedying the lack, *then the primary object of the pre-schizoid phase can only represent completeness, abundance. There is no primary object as the representation of lack.*

The primary object of the phase before object constancy is thus the *preambivalent object*. There is no representation other than this. Therefore, the pre-schizoid phase, by its very nature, possesses an explicit dynamic disposition to transfigure the primary object into the representation of an optimum, endowing it with the maximum conceivable force and power within the realm of object relations. It is crucial to bear this in mind in reference to subsequent developments.

Incidentally, one might label this primary positing of the object as the positively given as the fundamental affirmation, sustaining life in its psychic dimension.

Thus, the functional level of the pre-schizoid constitution of personality encompasses an ego experience and an experience of the primary object that are unconditional, comprehensive, and, in this sense, absolute, taking place in a timeless dimension. The line of reasoning I present aims to demonstrate that the object is included in this constitution due to the specific circumstances of the pre-schizoid phase – namely, the simultaneous and equal birth of ego and object in the act of perception – without leading to a conditionedness of the ego. Furthermore, the object of the pre-schizoid phase not only cannot be negated but represents absolute completeness and abundance, the absence of any lack. It is the preambivalent object. The negative is not yet representable as an object and is present in psychic space only as the pressure of anxiety urging a change in the existing overall situation.

The total package of these characteristics bestows upon this earliest layer of mental ontogenesis an ongoing dynamic, radiating potential, as the mental apparatus preserves all ontogenetic layers of its functioning and keeps them simultaneously active. The constitution of the pre-schizoid phase establishes a powerful experience of wholeness, perfection, and omnipotence, which can serve as both the foundation and reference point for a mystical longing for retrospection and, on the psychopathological level, the fixation and attraction point of a correspondingly powerful regressive tendency. In any case, however, the pre-schizoid phase would not be regarded as an objectless phase in the sense of primary narcissism.

In my perspective, thus, the death drive is not to be understood as a striving for the abolition of biological life as a consequence of the goal "to undo connections and thus to destroy things" (Freud 1938 in "An Outline of Psychoanalysis," p. 148). What is deadly in the psychic sense rather arises from the unforeseen and unintended consequence of the ego's self-abolition in the fusional movement. Nevertheless, this fusional movement itself is an understandable and imperative consequence of life's primary concern for itself, on the psychic level. The death drive is fed by the hunger for life, by the desire to suspend lack.

Considering that the ego, from the onset of its existence, is subjected to an inescapable, elemental threat of annihilation in the pursuit of its legitimate goal – namely, to nullify the tension of unpleasure – one must describe the nature of the ego as *primarily traumatic*. The impetus of this traumatic quality is the motor for the further structural development directly resulting from it. In this sense, I view the structural development of the psychic apparatus as a consequence of the necessity to intercept, bind, and shape the death drive's fusional dynamics in a way that neutralizes its potential to threaten the dimension of the psychical. As I will elaborate, this is the psychobiological task of the Oedipus complex, which makes it not only, as per Freud's formulation, the central core of all neuroses but the central core of the psyche in general.

Clinical evidence supporting the existence of the pre-schizoid phase is to be seen in primary psychogenic encapsulated autism, as described by Frances Tustin – the earliest and most severe form of mental illness. According to Tustin, the central pathogenic moment here lies in the premature and traumatic experience of a not-me object, implying a premature and therefore traumatic encounter with separateness from the object. In my terms, this is the experience of a primary object actively resisting and evading the fusional claim of the ego. This happens through a catastrophic manifestation of the fusional fear overwhelming the ego, i.e., through the defensive activity of the life drive against the fusional movement of the death drive.

Through this fear, the desired for fusional object transforms into the withdrawing not-me object. This event shatters the illusion of omnipotent control over the object, which is essential for healthy development, in a traumatic manner. The withdrawing not-me object is the one that resists and denies the early ego's claim to absolute and unconditional omnipotence. This omnipotence must always be understood as *omnipotent control over the object* in the sense of the unconditional claim to fusion with the object as the representation of abundance and completeness. This is precisely what the not-me object denies and what makes it the object that traumatically withdraws, resulting in its foreclosure. The withdrawing not-me object is the closest the pre-schizoid phase gets to a representation of the negative. Thus, the psychodynamics of primary encapsulated autism is all about omnipotence of the ego and its traumatic negation. Omnipotence is the clue and key to primary autism.

According to Tustin, the experience of the not-me object occurs in the very earliest days of life, perhaps interpartum or even still intrauterine, certainly before the establishment of the primal attachment, the primal bond. In reaction to this experience, the primary autistic child forecloses the object. This foreclosure of the primary object, and the consequent failure to establish attachment to the human object, results in the abortion of psychic development before its very inception. This catastrophic manifestation of the life drive, expressing itself so catastrophically due to an imminent danger of fusion, takes on the character of a psychic accident, underscoring the critical importance of binding the destructive potential of the death drive. The entire further psychic structure formation revolves around this point.

Tustin and others (Haag 1985, Haag et al. 2005, Winnicott 1949, Bick 1968, 1986) have detailed the severe existential fears faced by autistic children: dissolving, liquefying, leaking, falling to pieces, falling forever, having no skin or a skin full of holes, having the skin torn away, burning, freezing, suffocating, losing the sense of time and space, of orientation, losing a part or parts of the body. Joshua Durban (2017) refers to them as "anxieties of being." These are traumatic fears that arise when attempting to realize the fusional desire, expressing the peril of extinguishing the dimension of the psychical itself. They are the expression of the decay of the object representation, either in fusion itself or in the autistic foreclosure of the object.

Crucially, this is not a psychodynamic against the backdrop of object splitting; the pivotal moment lies in the withdrawal of the object from the omnipotence claim of the ego. Moreover, the fundamental foreclosure of the primary object, as it causally underpins the clinical picture, can only be conceived as a global and total one if it results in such a complete arrest of psychic development before the moment of primal attachment. This implies that such foreclosure is possible only in a phase preceding the onset of object splitting – i.e., in the pre-schizoid phase. After the onset of splitting, there would always be an aspect of the object that remains outside the foreclosure. Consequently, the encapsulation form of infantile autism must be regarded as clinical evidence for the existence of a pre-schizoid phase dominated by an unsplit, preambivalent primary object perceived as the source of all goodness.

An important consideration in this context is that experience in the pre-schizoid phase is intrinsically tied to and identical with immediate sensory experience, as this earliest experience arises directly from the perceptual function. The ability to distance oneself from immediate sensory experience only emerges through the capability to compare successive object representations in time, i.e., through object constancy. This ability to distance from immediate sensory experience is the prerequisite for any kind of symbol formation in the fundamental sense of forming mental contents that are not identical with sensory experience. By foreclosing the representation of the primary object, the psychogenic encapsulated autist cannot take this developmental step to compare object representations in time and thus remains trapped in being bound to the sensory. This, in turn, shapes the specific phenomenology of primary autistic symptomatology and conditions the difficult accessibility of these children, as described by authors such as Frances Tustin, Didier Houzel, Maria Rhode, Joshua

Durban, Anne Alvarez, Marie-Christine Laznik and others. The fact that primary encapsulation autism is bound to the sensory modality thus preserves the functional mode of the pre-schizoid phase and, in this sense, serves as additional evidence for the existence of such a phase.

In our context, focused on basic structural development, it is essential to emphasize that object constancy brings about a first dramatic *change in the mental level of functioning* by overcoming the binding to the immediate sensory system. The phenomenology of primary encapsulated autism attests to how profound this change is. With object constancy, the transition from the pre-schizoid phase to the infantile paranoid-schizoid position occurs. This transition represents a fundamental change in the level of functioning, similar to the transformation brought about later by the depressive position in overcoming the paranoid object split.

In summary, these considerations compel us to acknowledge the existence of a heretofore undiscovered earliest phase of psychic experiencing and functioning, crucial for the psychoanalytic explanation of psychogenic primary encapsulation autism. This phase involves unconscious structural phantasms directly arising from the imperatives of the perceptual function, possessing the character of Laws of Nature that constitute the psychical dimension and shape further structural development. Temporally, the beginning of this phase is still within the intrauterine form of existence.

In the bad, persecuting split object of the paranoid-schizoid position, several psychic movements converge: Firstly, the new capacity for object splitting, mediated by object constancy, allows the expression of deprivation – the aversive experience of need tension – as a negative object representation. Secondly, this bad object assumes the phantasmatic quality of the devouring object, symbolizing the

15

danger of ego dissolution linked to the fusional movement toward the object. Thirdly, this devouring quality is reinforced by the projection of the ego's devouring phantasies onto the primary object, serving as the oral expression of the fusional movement.

The transition to the depressive infantile position unfolds, as described by Melanie Klein, wherein the child, amid progressive cortical maturation and experiential development, begins to question its paranoid split reality. Traumatically, it realizes that its aggression directed at the bad object also harms and potentially annihilates the good object. In the dynamics of drives I have delineated, the child navigates this dilemma not merely through the confrontation with guilt and its reparative effort as well as through its experience of the indestructibility of the good object. Rather, it undergoes a distinctive developmental leap: under the pressure of the recurrent depressive crises, the ego evolves the capacity to stand observantly beside itself and to calm itself in the current crisis. This process of self-observation implies as such a splitting of the ego within itself.

I term this state the 'position of the ego outside the drive phantasm'. It signifies the introduction of the third element to the dichotomy of ego and primary object. This marks *the inception of the Oedipus complex*. From this position of the ego outside the drive phantasm, the father imago evolves, representing the exemplary non-mother object – an experience or dynamic effect, which is not in the direct genealogy of the primary object. The father imago unfolds subsequently through the psychic elaboration of the gender difference. Notably, this position alters the defensive landscape. The significance of the position of the ego outside the drive phantasm and, by extension, of the father imago is, against the background of the antagonism of the drives, that the splitting of the object is now no longer the only means of protecting the ego from the danger of fusion. Rather, this protection will be provided in the future by the self-reflective splitting of the ego within itself, out of which the ego, as long as it is observing itself, can no longer get lost in a fusional movement, since the observing part remains outside the fusion, which obeys the law of 'all-or-nothing'. The splitting of the object as the form of defense against the death drive is thus replaced by a splitting of the ego and becomes dynamically obsolete.

I suggest considering this split within the ego – the position outside – as the central acquisition and structural outcome of the depressive position because the overcoming of the splitting of the object results from it.

To simplify language, I will abbreviate the term `position of the ego outside the drive phantasm` and speak of the `position outside`.

The core of the father imago, in this position outside and the accompanying ego split, lies in the ego's self-reflective non-identity with itself. The father imago embodies this non-identity, symbolizing the structural ability and power to overcome paranoid object splitting. It stands as the personal embodiment of this self-reflective function. Consequently, the father imago is a derivative of the ego, representing its from now on central self-reflective function. This implies an unconditional structural separation of the father imago from the ego, as this separation expresses and structurally consolidates the self-reflective split of the ego. It incorporates an absolute prohibition directed at the ego, preventing it from equating itself with the father imago to appropriate its power. Such identification would annul the self-reflective non-identity of the ego, the functional principle of the father imago.

Borderline pathology, as a nosological category, is defined by the attack on and transgression of this prohibition, the consequent erosion of the father imago, and the resurgence of the good-bad split of the object imago – especially as proximity to the object intensifies, heightening the threat of fusional phantasy. The prohibition against equating ego and father imago becomes the fixation point of borderline development. Identity diffusion, characteristic of the borderline constitution, reflects the extensive use of the mechanism of projective identification, undermining the actual separateness of ego and object. In the background, the negation of the position outside – the negation of the position of the third – plays the pivotal role.

I will briefly outline the key structural implications of the position outside: firstly, the position outside, which denotes the reflective distance of the ego from itself and is encoded in the father imago, serves as precondition for the capacity to form symbols and for language development, as this reflective distance is crucial for *indexical designation*. As the position outside and, consequently, the symbolizing function are not yet present at the level of the infantile paranoid-schizoid position, there is a resulting tendency to bind the splitting imagination to immediate acting out and concretistic projective identification.

In the event of the collapse of the position outside, the symbolic function also falters, giving way to symbolic equation (Segal 1957, 1978). The ongoing, lifelong conflictual oscillation between the paranoid-schizoid and depressive modes of functioning underscores the perpetual need for elaborating the position outside and, by extension, the father imago. The realm of the symbolic is not a static acquisition but demands continual work effort and maintenance.

Secondly, the developmental leap to the position outside, by overcoming object splitting, traverses the boundary of the structurally psychotic organization of the psyche. This threshold to self-determined and rational existence thus consists in the self-reflective splitting of the ego and is guarded by the father imago as precisely the representation of the reflective non-identity of the ego with itself.

Thirdly, with the overcoming of the splitting of the object by the position outside, the ego attains access to reality as a secured dimension since reality presupposes not a split but a unified object conception. Access to this unsplit spatiotemporal identity of the object was not yet structurally attainable under a condition of psychic functioning characterized by the good-bad split of object representation as the regulatory mode of the drives, precisely because of the split of the object. This access to reality via the discovery of the spatiotemporal identity of the object is also associated with the differentiation between inside and outside, inner world and outer reality.

Indeed, this implies that, on the level of the unconscious structural phantasies, father imago, self-reflective capacity, and access to reality are, in fact, identical.

In clinical psychosis, characterized by a loss of access to reality, regression follows this specific trajectory: The elimination of the position outside results, on one hand, in the collapse of the father imago and, on the other hand, in the eradication of the distinction between inner and outer reality as a symptom of reverting to the good-bad split of the object imago. This return to the good-bad split involves the forfeiture of the spatiotemporal identity of the object, precisely leading to the loss of access to reality and, with it, loss of distinction between inner and outer reality. The annulment of the demarcation between inner and outer reality precipitates the central symptomatology of psychosis – hallucination and delusion. The object-imagination in psychosis is rooted in the genealogy of the imago of the primary object that persists as the sole type of representation in psychic space after the collapse of the father imago and its associated representations.

This concludes the discussion on the position outside. The pre-schizoid phase, paranoid-schizoid, and depressive positions delineate the stages of object constitution, running parallel to psychosexual development. While I consistently referred to good and bad split objects, their representation has long been organized into part objects – the imagines of the good and bad breast. The formation of these part objects ties the imagination of the primary object to the oral mode of biologically determined psychosexuality.

With this step, the initial representation of the primary object, which comprised the mere temporal contiguity of a complex sensory stimulation converging in the central nervous system simultaneously, has now bound itself to the manifestation of corporal sexuality. This marks the establishment of a power junction that propels further psychic development. Specifically, it denotes that the imago of the primary object, initially sought for fusion by the primary ego as the source of relief from all unpleasure, *is now equated and identified with the object of sexual pleasure.*

This is the metapsychological formulation of primal attachment. This equation and attachment, constitutive of the human condition, does not occur only in the most severe form of psychic pathology, the encapsulation form of psychogenic infantile autism. It marks the commencement of the oral phase of psychosexual development.

With the acquisition of the position outside and the thus given access to reality, this part object of the good and, subsequently, of the bad breast now experiences a suspension of its internal split and is thus clearly localized in reality. It becomes the *reality breast.*

These considerations yield implications for the theory of the depressive position. According to John Steiner (1993, "Psychic Retreats"), the mourning process in response to the crisis of the depressive position, following Freud (1917, "Mourning and Melancholia"), involves two steps. First, in the immediate reaction to the loss, there is a denial of this loss and an attempt to internally preserve and possess and protect the object, which ultimately proves futile in the experience that the ego cannot do this. The second step of the mourning process, according to Steiner, involves recognizing the loss and acknowledging the existence of the object independent of the ego. This presents a situation where, due to the conflictual complications of the depressive position, the independence and autonomy of the object are acknowledged.

Considering this formulation against the backdrop of my reflections on the content and dynamics of the two psychic drives, it becomes evident that something even more fundamental is transpiring than outlined in in the already heavyweight formulations of the classical conception. For the first time, the ego is compelled to realize that its previous pact with the death drive in the pursuit of fusional unity with the object is not inherently self-evident, natural, good, and right. Quite the contrary, the life-sustaining object has been severely damaged, perhaps even destroyed, in the pursuit of this goal, on the level of the drive phantasies.

Hence, a definite prohibition confronts the ego for the first time in its collaboration with the death drive, challenging the initially perceived naturalness of such collaboration. The crisis of the depressive position serves as a prefiguration of the later crisis of the oedipal conflict, anticipating the castration threat and the incest prohibition. *In this crisis of the depressive position, the theme of a necessary separation, of separateness of ego and object, is expressed and psychically apprehended for the first time.*

The overall process of psychic structuration can be viewed as one in which the separation of the ego from the object is to be established. Ultimately, this separation is the fundamental task of the Oedipus complex. This structural separation is the basis of psychic life, insofar as the act of perception from which the dimension of the psychical emerges is based on the separation, the separateness of ego and object. Thus, the separation of ego and object is also the basis of mental health; conversely, the striving to abolish this separation is the fundamental motive of any kind of mental pathology.

With the recognition of separation from the object, the narcissistic relation to the object transitions into an objective one. Under the influence of the death drive, characterized by the fusion phantasy, the object is perceived as an extension of the ego, that is, it is narcissistically cathected. Only with the resolution of the developmental task of the depressive position does the object assume its place in psychic space in its own right. Consequently, themes such as cognition and truth acquire significance, as they pertain to the object's inherent nature. The death drive, by its very essence, is directed against cognition and truth as it is opposing the separate identity of the object, while the enforcement of separation from the object and access to cognition and truth is propelled by the life drive, by Eros.

I have just phrased this in a way that suggests the crisis of the depressive position serves to illuminate for the ego that its inherent interest, namely, to maintain the relationship to the life-sustaining object, does not align with the fusionary and insofar de-objectalizing goal of the death drive. I approached this as if ego and death drive had been in a coalition, an alliance of sorts, until this point, as the contradiction between its own nature and that of the death drive had not yet dawned on the ego. However, it is crucial to bear in mind that in the earliest condition, wherein the primary ego, in a state of lack, seeks to incorporate the primary object, the ego is identical with the death drive. *Intrinsically, the ego of the pre-schizoid phase is the death drive.*

Hence, the ego would not disengage from the death drive as a distinct motivational structure until the crisis of the depressive position. In other words, what we subsequently refer to as the death drive would denote the early functional manifestation of the ego, where the ego was entirely ruthless towards the object, with its sole focus on alleviating the tensions of need and, in this sense, achieving the state of bliss. Consequently, what we label as the drive in the psychic realm would retain the force of globality and totality, of timelessness of the pre-schizoid phase.

In essence, we have fallen into the trap of reification by labeling the force we term the death drive in this way, thereby preventing ourselves from recognizing that the death drive is the preserved functional form of the primary ego. The reason for this is likely rooted in the tremendous dynamic force and, so to speak, wildness inherently associated with the death drive, which unavoidably makes the classification as a drive seem inevitable.

II

Beyond the Pleasure Principle

Insofar, then, as I have introduced the death drive as the impulse towards fusion with the gratifying object, which entails the peril of ego dissolution, it becomes imperative to examine whether a theory of the life and death drives is inherently situated beyond the pleasure principle. The question arises as to my justification in ascribing to the death drive a significance divergent from Freud's established definition. Scientifically speaking, such justification is only warranted if Freud's derivation is theoretically refuted.

Freud, who basically saw in the death drive the drive to self-destruction, writes in "The Economic Problem of Masochism": "The libido has the task of making the destroying instinct innocuous, and it fulfills the task by diverting that instinct to a great extent outwards - soon with the help of a special organic system, the muscular apparatus - towards objects in the external world" (1924, p. 163).

For Freud, then, the death drive was associated with the goal of destruction, as a consequence of the workload and thus the unpleasure associated with maintaining a multicellular organism. The object of this destructive drive for Freud is therefore the self of the subject insofar as this self is the cause of unpleasure, of the unlust. Consequently, life, according to Freud, was only sustainable when this death drive was redirected from the self "towards objects in the external world". This, then, involves a change of object, away from the self to the external objects.

In contrast, I posit that the death drive is inherently directed, *from the outset*, towards the *inner* object – specifically against the separateness of the ego from the representation of the primary object, against the necessary separation of subject and object of perception. The aim of the death drive is the suspension of the tension of unpleasure by fusion with the object, attributing to the object the capability to suspend any state of deficiency. This goal has nothing to do with primary aggression aimed at the self. Psychic life is constituted by the relation of the ego to the object. There is no objectless primary phase in which aggression would be directed towards the self.

This insight leads to the crucial theoretical understanding that the apparent turn of the death drive to the external results from the ego gaining access to reality through overcoming the splitting of the object. I have previously illustrated that the good-bad split of the object in the infantile paranoid-schizoid and depressive positions serves as a defense mechanism against the death drive by preventing fusion through the splitting of the object. I have explained that this initial mode of defense is supplanted by the self-reflective splitting of the ego, which is the structural resolution of the conflict of the depressive position by overcoming the splitting of the object. The splitting of the ego now assumes the same function that the splitting of the object had before, namely, to prevent the fusion of the ego with the object. For fusion requires the all-or-nothing principle. By splitting the ego, a part of the ego always remains outside the fusion, just as before, by splitting the object, a part of the object always remained outside the fusional movement. I have termed this self-reflective splitting of the ego the position of the ego outside the drive phantasm, or in short, the position outside.

It is crucial to emphasize that the formulation of the position of the ego outside the drive phantasm involves not only a structural process – substituting the splitting of the object with the splitting of the ego as the defense mechanism against the desire for fusion – but also signifies that the ego is no longer in seamless identity with the drive phantasm. To clarify, this demarcates the difference between the psychotic or hallucinatory form of experience and the non-psychotic form. Alternatively, one could express this as the transition from an animistic-hallucinatory experience of the world to a state marked by the position outside the drive phantasm and the self-reflective splitting of the ego.

Through this innovation of the position outside, the previously purely intrapsychic, subjectively defined imago of the primary object is brought into congruence with the representation of the external real object. For, on the one hand, the real object is not split along a good-bad dichotomy, making reality inaccessible under the object's splitting constitution. On the other hand, access to reality depends on the ego's ability to step out of hallucination.

Before as after, the death drive is directed to the object, but this object is at first the primary, subjective – *inner* – object of the pre-schizoid phase and of the split condition of the object in the infantile paranoid-schizoid and depressive positions. Later, with the position of the ego outside the drive phantasm, external reality becomes recognizable and to be perceived as such, allowing the death drive to be explicitly directed towards the external, real object. This shift seems like a transition from the inside to the outside, but it is, in fact, the result of the discovery of the dimension of external reality.

The quality and the object, the content and the aim of the death drive does not change in any way by this turning outside, in particular there is no change from autoaggression to heteroaggression, i.e. no change of object. A consequential theoretical misunderstanding lies here, as the death drive only because of this erroneous assumption of an object change could be equated with destruction, which – according to Freud – would enforce this object change in order to prevent the self-destruction of the subject. In this way, Freud had failed to recognize that this drive fundamentally targets neither the self nor the object but rather the moment of separation. The death drive is not inherently the "destroying instinct" (op.cit.). The aggression associated with the fusional death drive pertains to the control, subjugation, exploitation, and incorporation of the object, insofar as the object is regarded as the repository of all that is good. It is directed in the same sense toward both the inner and the outer object.

Regarding terminology, it is more accurate to speak of the intrapsychic object concerning the primary relation to the object. The term "inner object" implies a counter-terminus of the outer object, not yet given at this early stage but conceptualized only with access to reality. Thus, the term "inner object" is applicable only ex post facto, with this caveat maintained here for simplicity.

Freud would not have accepted today's common reduction of the death drive to a general innate aggression. He deemed it theoretically insufficient to speak of an aggressive drive without indicating the necessity within the subject from which such primary aggression arises. For him, this necessity lay in the work demand of maintaining a multicellular living being and the associated unlust that leads to the desire for the dissolution of this multicellular organization. The "destroying instinct" would then be deflected outward with the implication of object change to ensure life maintenance. However, with the absence of object change, this derivation of the death drive is no longer tenable. That this erroneous assumption could occur results from the fact that at the time of Freud's theorizing on the death drive, the concept of the inner, purely phantasmatically constituted object had not yet existed. He did not know of this inner object, being brought into congruence with the outer object in a specific phantasmatic process – the infantile paranoid-schizoid and depressive positions. This was possible only through Melanie Klein's discoveries. As it were at his time, it actually looked as if the death drive was deflected from the inside to the outside.

Without this implication of an inevitable change of object, Freud's concept of the death drive lacks its axiomatic derivation. The genesis of aggression cannot be derived from a goal of the death drive in self-destruction. The absence of object change renders this derivation untenable. The aggressive relation to the explicitly external object does not result from a change in the drive's object. Rather, it represents an expansion of the existing object relation, from the inner to the outer, external object. As a consequence of this circumstance, aggression loses the central significance it would have if the question of being or non-being of the subject were connected with its external deflection. It is not the center of the death drive.

Nevertheless, Freud's fundamental insight into the necessity of a dualistic conception of the drive remains valid. Interestingly, Freud's formulations on the death drive and mine are not as distant as one might initially assume. For Freud, the cause of the death drive was the unpleasure associated with maintaining a multicellular organism. Similarly, in my perspective, unpleasure or lack serves as the cause of the death drive. While Freud posits that unpleasure leads to the goal of the subject's destruction, I argue that the desire for fusion with the object, where the means to suspend any state of lack are located, arises from unpleasure. Insofar as fusion, if realized, however would result in the annulment of the dimension of the psychical as such, in my view one also ends up with self-destruction, but on a distinctly different path than Freud.

I will demonstrate that a modified theory of the death drive, such as I propose, is capable of formulating a general theory of psychoanalysis in terms of a metapsychology based on consistent principles throughout.

Instincts and their Vicissitudes

With this, I propose a novel conceptualization of the drive. From the primary hypothesis of the genesis of the psychical from the perceptual function, i.e. from the confrontation of the primary ego with the primary object, I have derived the conclusion that there is a first phase in psychic development not as yet described – the pre-schizoid phase. In this phase, neuronal capacity has yet to mature sufficiently to maintain an object representation stably for comparison with temporally subsequent representations. I have termed this the capacity for object constancy.

Object constancy serves as the foundation for both memory and the perception of time. Likewise, it underlies the ability to perceive space, encompassing the recognition of distance and three-dimensionality. The emergence of spatial perception results from the *sequence* of the momentary representations of the primary object in object constancy. Thus, in the phase preceding the acquisition of object constancy, perception is two-dimensional, akin to the distanceless adhesive contact with surfaces experienced by primary psychogenic autists, whose disease-causing traumatization occurred in precisely this first phase of psychic development and whose functional mode remained fixated on this level.

The cognitive categories of space and time, therefore, emanate from object constancy. In other words, within the framework of this first level of psychic functioning before object constancy, we are in an experience outside of space and time. It is mainly this characteristic that makes the forms of primary autism located in this stage so difficult to understand and to access. To complete the picture, it is essential to add that without the dimensions of space and time, the ability to relate to other bodies is not possible. The absence of space and time means that the object *as an other body* cannot be conceptualized, rendering primal attachment unattainable. This is the situation of the psychogenic primary encapsulated autists.

In this condition, where the comparison of representations and internal states is not yet feasible, the ego is confronted with a solipsistic object, which is literally the universe, the All where nothing exists beyond it. Associated with this primary constitution is an experience that, due to the lack of comparability, is total, global, and timeless. Reality is of course not yet accessible, and the ego is perceived as omnipotent, as it lacks any conditioning. Simultaneously, the object is seen as the representation of absolute abundance and completeness, since in a state where only the respectively activated primary object exists, the potential for the suspension of lack or deficiency is exclusively attributed to this object, which therefore is precisely everything, the All.

The theme on both the ego and the object side is paradoxically absoluteness, as no insight into the conditionality of reality is yet possible. This paradox arises because, despite the child being objectively in a state of maximum dependence and helplessness at this early stage – seemingly contradictory to the experience of absoluteness, omnipotence, and unlimited abundance – the lack of insight into conditionality fosters an experience of absoluteness as the primary psychological condition. It is this contradiction that has made it so difficult to conceptualize this earliest constitution. While the body may be shaken by organismic despair, a traumatic experience of lack, on the psychic level, this lack, in the context of an experience of the primary object as the embodiment of absolute good, generates an acute phantasy of fusion. This, in turn, gives rise to the panic of ego-loss. Thus, this panic is not a direct response to the organismic deficiency; rather, this notion of a direct response to organismic deficiency ignores a crucial phantasmatic intermediate step – the fusional phantasy. This missing element introduces the entire issue of psychic processing.

As mentioned earlier, object splitting is not achievable in this state, as it requires object constancy. The ability to neuronally sustain successive object representations is the precondition for psychically maintaining the counter-image to the split imago. Therefore, I term this primary state of the psyche the pre-schizoid phase.

Contrary to Freud's assumption that the tremendous power and archaic characteristics of the two drives stem from a biological origin, in my view they actually originate from a phase of psychic development – precisely the pre-schizoid phase –, which, as said, is entirely unconditioned, lacking both space and time, and in which, in particular, reality still remains beyond any psychic comprehensibility. The power and dynamic force of the drives manifest as expression and consequence of this fundamental lack of any condition.

The archaic characteristics of the drives, instead of having a biological descent, arise from the pre-schizoid phase being tethered to an immediate, two- and one-dimensional sensory system, akin to the experience of primary autists, who remain fixated on this primary form of perception. These archaic characteristics represent the residue of a primitive primary-process relation to the body, a consequence of being bound to a sensory experience devoid of any form of distancing due to the absence of object constancy. Importantly, these archaic traits do not stem from a biological rooting of the drives.

Given that the pre-schizoid phase spans a brief period – only a few weeks from the intrauterine onset of cortical perceptual function to postpartum at the time of object constancy and primal attachment – it might be surprising that the drives draw their quasi-inexhaustible energetic potential from such a limited timeframe. However, the drives, in their unconditional nature, mirror the unconditionality of the pre-schizoid phase and maintain its mode of functioning, aligning with the principle that the psyche keeps all ontogenetic layers of its structure and function alive and simultaneously active.

It is crucial to realize the radical nature of this proposition: the pre-schizoid phase, representing the earliest and most archaic mode of experience, is an actual presence within each of us. The drives serve as the living expression of this presence.

The influence of the pre-schizoid phase is fundamentally determined by the feature of absoluteness in its internal phantasmatic constitution. This constitution is devoid of any conditions tied to reality; it is total, global, outside of time and space. To draw a comparison, the pre-schizoid phase can be likened to an atomic power plant that energetically fuels and sustains the psyche. In conserving the pre-schizoid phase, the two drives precisely encapsulate this dynamic potential.

In any case, the contents and processes of the pre-schizoid phase remain permanently unconscious due to the inherent unconsciousness associated with this phase. This unconsciousness stems from the absence of the ego's capacity to distance itself from its own experience. This essential feature significantly contributes to the powerful and pervasive force of the two drives. The primary reason for this lies in the absence of object constancy, indicating the not yet developed ability to compare object representations over time. Object constancy serves as the foundation and prerequisite for any capability to distance oneself from one's own experience.

In my interpretation, the drives represent the two distinct states of *the ego of the pre-schizoid phase*. The development of object constancy removes the immediate experiential actuality from these archaic ego constitutions. With the newfound ability for a good-bad split in the representation of the object, the psyche transitions into another functional mode, specifically that of the paranoid-schizoid position. Due to the principle of preserving all ontogenetic structures and functions that have ever been part of psychic actuality, these original archaic ego states persist. Given that they pertain to a mode beyond space and time, outside the experience of conditionality, these latter determinants contribute to their self-encapsulated yet highly energetic constitution, leading to their characterization as the drives.

Therefore, the pre-schizoid ego, under the dominance of the phantasy of fusion, is the death drive, and the primordial ego opposing fusion is the life drive. The drives are not external, such as biological forces acting on the psychic space consisting of the relation between ego and object. Instead, they are the archaic forces that arise from and constitute *this relation of ego and object itself*: on one hand, the desire for fusion, and on the other, the opposition and defense against it.

In summary, the distinct drive character of both ego constitutions, or simply both drives, is rooted on the structural level in the fact that, during this early stage, the ego remains completely in an unbroken identity with the phantasm of desire as well as the phantasm of fear due to the absence of object constancy. This absence results from the not yet developed comparison of states; perspectives of time and space, distance, and three-dimensionality do not yet exist. On the other hand, the dynamic aspect comes, as mentioned earlier, from the unconditioned and absolute nature of the pre-schizoid phase.

With this, I also propose a different fundamental concept of energy: The energetic force of the drives does not arise from a plethora of energetic cathexis or charge, thought of in quantitative terms. Instead, it stems from the structural origin of the drives, originating from a state of absolute unconditionality, i.e., the absence of being bound to any kind of condition. Thus, it is a structural concept of psychic energy or, better, charge, grounded in logical causality, much like – revisiting the metaphor – atomic energy.

For the sake of completeness, it should be added that the realm of instincts rooted in the corporeal – whether classical sexuality or Panksepp's basic emotions and Solms' neurobiological drives – protrudes into the psychical as an inner external world, so to speak. It is treated and experienced by the psychic drives within the framework of their own thematicity and intentionality, as I have described them. This behaves no differently here than it does for sexuality within Freud's third drive theory. The essential point is that the psychic drives have an exclusively psychic genesis and an efficacy developing exclusively from the psychical.

The life drive condition of the pre-schizoid ego – and thus precisely the life drive – has a double face in this context: on the one hand, as fear, expressing the danger of fusional ego dissolution, and on the other hand, as the moment containing the security of the ego. This security is connected with the object expressly separated from the ego, inasmuch as separation from the object excludes fusion. Good mothering conveys to the child precisely this sense of the life drive-related security of his ego. This is achieved by combining empathic attunement to the child's states and needs with the expression of the mother's secure separateness.

When I speak of omnipotence as the leitmotif of the pre-schizoid phase with reference to the drives, this is not meant primarily as a description of an experience but as a description of a structural fact. In a world consisting only of the primary ego and the primary object, and which – before object constancy, i.e., before the ability to compare an object representation with a preceding one – is not yet conditioned by anything, the ego faces the seeming possibility of incorporating, in fusion with the object, the annulment of any deficiency. The pre-schizoid phase therefore contains, *as a structure*, the seeming possibility of the ego expanding itself into the egocosmic ego. I therefore see the pre-schizoid phase, structurally, as the position of omnipotence. Omnipotence is the structural characteristic of this world. The unconditional, absolute power of the drives is the result of this omnipotence.

Again, as above with reference to Melanie Klein and the inner, subjective object, the historical situation must be taken into account. In Freud's time, a pre-schizoid phase that emerges autonomously from the perceptual function was not yet conceivable. It is therefore not surprising if Freud regarded the drives as coming from an outside of the psychical, precisely from the biological. The pre-schizoid phase is indeed an outside of the introspectively directly accessible world due to its essential unconsciousness, which, as mentioned before, arises from the lack of any possibility of distancing of the ego from its own experience.

The Ego and the Id

The subsequent inquiry revolves around the origin of the id and the question of the unconscious. In the context of the established theory of mental instances, the id serves as the unconscious drive pole of the personality, and its contents constitute the psychic manifestation of these drives. The other instances – namely, the ego and the superego – differentiate themselves from the id, which is postulated to be primary. Conversely, I posit that the primary ego, emerging from perception, opens the psychic space in its polar opposition to the primary object as the object of perception. In this perspective, the id would not be primary. This provokes an exploration into the way through which the id comes into operation.

The previous good-bad split of the object in the infantile paranoid-schizoid and depressive positions is incompatible and clashes with the emerging spatiotemporal unity of the object. This unity, or the unsplit conception of the object, arises from the resolution of the crisis of the depressive position. The newfound spatiotemporal unity of the object allows access to reality, as reality necessitates a unified conception of the object. The real object, as said, is not divided along a good-bad dichotomy. The spatiotemporal unity of the object is made possible by the self-reflective splitting of the ego, occurring in the position outside.

From this juncture, the splitting of the ego takes precedence over the splitting of the object as the primary defense mechanism against the desire for fusion, rendering the latter obsolete.

The self-reflective splitting of the ego represents a crucial developmental milestone, specifically involving a retreat from the pursuit of omnipotent, fusional control over the object. This pivotal step towards self-reflection becomes feasible only through the relativization of this fusional desire and the associated work of mourning. Behind the splitting of the ego, in this sense, is the working through of the entire conflict of the depressive position.

It is crucial to recognize that these represent two entirely opposite modes of ego functioning: in one scenario, the ego remains unswervingly identical to the drive phantasm; in the other, the ego assumes a reflective distance from the drive. The former mode of ego identification with the drive phantasm is linked to object splitting as defense mechanism against the death drive and, consequently, lacks access to the reality dimension of the world. To emphasize, this operational mode characterizes the ego in psychosis.

Due to the incompatibility of these two operational modes of the ego, the earlier functional mode tied to splitting of the object and the associated mode of experience now become unconscious. Through this process, the dimension of the psychogenic unconscious originates within the psyche. This marks the inception of primal repression (Urverdrängung), leading to the structurally unconscious as the core of the id. Therefore, the quality of unconsciousness here is not inherently tied to the drives, as in the classical model of the psychic instances, but rather arises from the incompatibility of the ego states. Considering that the crisis of the infantile depressive position occurs temporally between the fourth and sixth month of life, this, according to my interpretation, would roughly mark the birth of the id as instance of the psychic apparatus. Intriguingly, this aligns with the birth moment of the father imago through the position outside, at least in terms of its structural foundation – the position of the third.

The previous mode of functioning of the psyche, tethered to the ego's identity with the drive phantasm and consequently to the good-bad split of the object, is not discarded with the transition to the self-reflective split of the ego. Instead, it persists in that operational mode of the ego where the ego does not distance itself from itself; in other words, where the self-reflective split of the ego is not in operation. Nevertheless, this identity mode of ego function is no longer accessible to the self-reflective ego of the ego split. It constitutes a categorically different mode of experience, and this is precisely why this mode of the identity of the ego with the drive phantasm is unconscious in the structural sense.

This implies that not only the pre-schizoid phase but also the original infantile paranoid-schizoid and depressive positions remain unconscious in the genuine sense, since they are genetically prior to the time of the position outside. Our later understanding of paranoid-schizoid and depressive conflicts is derived from the subsequent descendants of the primary infantile conflicts, emerging within the framework of the later circular repetition processes.

Conversely, consciousness or awareness can be defined as the self-reflective operation of the ego outside the drive phantasm, based on a splitting of the ego. Considering that the self-reflective splitting of the ego necessitates a continuous effort, a work demand, one might assert that the condition of identity with the drive phantasm is always the basal functional form of the ego.

In essence, it must be assumed that the ego is constantly perceiving in two different and mutually incompatible modalities, only one of which is directly conscious.

This statement carries significant implications for our understanding of the broader landscape of psychic life. For instance, when relating dreams to the identity of the ego with the drive phantasm, it becomes plausible to assert that we are likely in a perpetual state of dreaming, with the dream layer during wakefulness being superimposed by the ego's self-reflective mode. Similarly, the delineation of these two concurrent ego modalities has consequences for discussions on the creative aspect of the psyche. It suggests that this creative aspect is potentially nurtured by the identity dimension of ego experience, particularly in its relation to the directly sensorial and to an extensive displacement of energies, as seen in the primary process.

The inherent incompatibility between the two functional modes of the ego gives rise to a further consideration regarding the genetic priority of the instances. As previously outlined, I establish the temporal precedence of the ego over the id based on the foundational assumption that the dimension of the psychical emerges from the unfolding of the poles of perception and perceived, where the perceiving instance is equated with the primary ego. However, in light of the above discussion, wherein the primary ego of identity with the drive phantasm transforms into the core of the id during the resolution of the conflict of the infantile depressive position, and resulting from the incompatibility with the new reflective ego mode becomes structurally unconscious, this formulation requires refinement.

To be more precise: There exist two fundamentally divergent functional modes of the ego, coexisting simultaneously. Yet, the genetically earlier mode lacks the capacity for self-reflection, by that remaining tethered to object splitting. Consequently, it does not meet the criterion of correspondence to reality and is, therefore, unconscious in relation to the now dominant new ego constitution.

This earlier mode transforms into the id, thereby constituting the quality of psychogenic unconsciousness.

As it turns out, then, the issue is somewhat more complicated: The new asset that emerges is not the id but the ego of the position outside, which is the bearer of the new dimension of consciousness. Through the emergence of this new dimension, the id constitutes itself as a separated instance. Thus, the id has in fact always existed and is the ego of identity with the drive phantasm, i.e. the ego of the pre-schizoid phase and of the primary splitting constitution of the infantile paranoid-schizoid and depressive positions. It is consequently also true that the id is the seat of the drives, insofar as the drives are, as said, the ego states of the pre-schizoid phase. Accordingly, the central difference to the classical view of the theory of instances is that I identify the id with the primary ego of identity with the drive phantasm. *The id is the early ego.*

This is also the underlying reason for the dissolution of the classical division of instances in psychosis. Psychosis, as previously noted, involves the ego regressing to identification with the drive phantasm, resulting in the splitting of object relation and, consequently, the loss of access to reality and the father imago. This regressive shift, where the ego relinquishes its secondary-process position outside of the drive phantasm, leads to the elimination of the separation between the id and the ego in terms of psychic instances. This separation is originally brought about by the position outside. In a parallel manner, the collapse of the father imago in psychosis leads to the loss of the superego characteristic of the structurally neurotic, oedipal level.

In the earlier discussion, I defined object constancy as the neuronal ability to sustain a representation over time and, from a psychological perspective, as the capacity to compare a current object representation with a previous one. I highlighted a significant shift in the functional level associated with the attainment of object constancy. On one hand, this achievement enables the establishment of the good-bad split of the object, necessitating the mental preservation of the counter-image of the split imago – thus, precisely, object constancy. On the other hand, the ability for comparison, facilitated by object constancy, liberates dependence on the immediate, distanceless sensorial mode of experience.

This marks the transition from the pre-schizoid phase to the paranoid-schizoid position.

With this transition, a situation arises where the existing pre-schizoid functional level of the ego shows to be incompatible with the newly introduced functional level of object splitting. The pre-schizoid phase constitutes a world of its own, characterized by timelessness, globality, and totality – a world where the ego indulges in the fiction of omnipotence, creating an egocosmic ego. It is dominated by an unsplit primary object, representing absolute abundance and completeness. However, as said, this structure proves incompatible with the good-bad split characteristic of the paranoid-schizoid position.

Hence, one can deduce that primal repression unfolds in two distinct stages. First, during the transition from the pre-schizoid phase to the infantile paranoid-schizoid position facilitated by object constancy, and subsequently, in the shift from object splitting to the reality-adapted spatiotemporal identity of the object through the position outside. Given that this later developmental step is linked to the self-reflective splitting of the ego within itself, marking the inception of consciousness and awareness, it represents the juncture where the id is segregated as a distinct instance of the psychic apparatus, as this id now bears the explicit quality of unconsciousness.

The id, therefore, comprises two strata: Initially, the earliest pre-schizoid functional level, in which the drives are rooted, followed by the infantile paranoid-schizoid and depressive functional level characterized by object splitting. Both functional levels of the id, however, remain bound by the shared attribute of the ego's identity with the drive phantasm – essentially, the absence of the self-reflective position outside and, consequently, the quality of unconsciousness. As a point of reference, it is worth noting that all pathologies within the autistic spectrum trace their origins to the pre-schizoid functional level.

The Oedipus Complex

The subsequent focus is on the oedipal constitution of the psyche and the Oedipus complex. With the emergence of the position outside, characterized by access to reality, the sensual experience of the real, along with the recognition of sex difference and sexuality linked to that difference, takes center stage as to psychic attention. In the earlier splitting world of the infantile paranoid-schizoid and depressive positions, the predominant theme was not gender but rather the dichotomy between good and bad. The psychic elaboration of the sexual-genital dynamics between the parents, known as the constitution of the Oedipus complex, becomes the central task in the ensuing developmental phases.

In the context of the aspects being discussed here, anality primarily involves, on one hand, the confrontation with the moment of control over the object through the voluntary motor system. On the other hand, the development of the concept of the means – specifically, the tool associated with the voluntary motor system – lays the groundwork for the imagination of the phallus.

Subsequently, at the oedipal stage, the notion of incest with the mother takes on the role of the imaginative representation for fusion with the object corresponding to this developmental level. Respected authors, expressly including Janine Chasseguet-Smirgel (passim; cf. 1975), have underscored this unconscious fusional significance of incest, noteworthy in both sexes. Bridging the conceptual gap from reflections on the primal constitution of the psyche and the circumstances within the resolution of the infantile depressive position, it is a substantial leap to view the fully developed oedipal conflict constellation as the expression of the same foundational drive dynamic, in which the ego, under the influence of the death drive, seeks to establish omnipotent control over the object, obliterate separation, and effectively fuse with it.

Nevertheless, an analysis of the oedipal conflict constellation reveals that the same themes and forces are at play here as those previously described in the context of overcoming the crisis of the infantile depressive position. The rationale for equating the conflict dynamics of the crisis of the infantile depressive position with those of the oedipal constellation stems from their structural and dynamic homogeneity. This, in turn, serves as evidence of an underlying and pervasive drive theme.

I will now digress on the significance of the mother and father image at the level of unconscious structural phantasms to elucidate the psychic background against which the imagination of the oedipal primal scene unfolds its narrative.

The representation of the mother involves the subsumption of all objectal experiences, which, over the course of development, converge with the original representation of the primary object. This transforms her into the imago, from which, following the acquisition of access to reality, the relationship to all other real objects emerges – essentially, the sum-total imago of the world.

It is crucial to recognize that I am discussing matters at the level of unconscious structural phantasms. By "mother," I mean that psychic imagination that takes shape from the representation of the primary object, representing its ongoing development or unfolding. However, the core of the imago "mother" lies in the primary object, which has nothing at all to do with the actual mother but is rather the precipitate and expression of the fact that the human perceptual function emerges precisely from the dichotomy of the perceiving ego and the perceived primary object.

To comprehend the significance of this concept, it is important to recall that the primary object in the earliest stages of mental development is entirely artificial. It arises from the different sensory afferents coincidentally reaching the perceptual centers of the cerebral cortex simultaneously and are then mapped and consolidated into a unified representation solely due to their simultaneous occurrence. This situation illustrates one of those instances where psychological predisposition and biological circumstances intersect. The biological mother, given her profound biological significance, naturally lends herself as the embodiment of the representation of the primary object.

The same principles apply to the father imago. As mentioned earlier, we encounter a situation where the core of the father imago involves a *function* centrally significant for human development – the self-reflective splitting of the ego and the resulting position of the ego outside the drive phantasm. Consequently, a psychodynamically highly effective new principle emerges, specifically the position of the third, which adds itself to the existing duality and opposition of ego and primary object. This introduces a specification and alteration of their relationship, marking the inception of the oedipal triangulation. It arises from and corresponds to the objectivizing nature of the psyche that, as an expression of this centrally important new function and

43

for its psychic anchoring, fixation, and bonding, the psyche seeks a personal, objectal expression. Within the sociological family structure, the father, in his capacity as non-mother figure, typically fulfills this role, aligning with the biological background.

Certainly, it is not insignificant for both individual and supra-individual cultural development whether a sociological structure exists that facilitates the seamless transfer of the autonomous psychogenic structural phantasms to actual father and mother figures or functions. A vital and straightforward formation of primal scene phantasmatization hinges on the ability to carry out this transfer without complications.

In this context, the primal scene assumes paramount psychic significance, as it represents the sexual union of the father with the mother, in which the father is not susceptible to the danger and anxiety of fusion. He embodies the antifusional principle itself, him originating from the position outside – that is, from the reflective non-identity of the ego with itself. In this sense, the imago of the primal scene serves as the phantasmatic definition of the life drive, specifically in representing the non-fusional relation with the mother. This power to banish fusional fear culminates in, and is represented by, the imago of the phallus as the means through which the father unites with the mother. The phallus is, therefore, inherently associated with the father. From the perspective of the death drive, the objective is to appropriate this phallic power, as ostensibly, within its protection, fusional incest can be consummated.

However, the phantasmatic usurpation of the apotropaic, protective phallus by the ego results in the collapse of its banishing power. This is because the father imago, and consequently the phallus, is bound by the imperative of non-identity with the ego. As explained, the structural and dynamic significance of the father imago arises from the reflective distancing of the ego from itself in the position outside – essentially, from the splitting of the ego that renders fusion impossible and, in turn, transcends paranoid object-splitting as defense mechanism against the death drive. The father is the personal embodiment of this position outside. Through the concretistic appropriation of the phallus, the separation between ego and father imago, and thus the splitting of the ego, the reflective non-identity of the ego with itself, would be undone. This signifies the psychic catastrophe of abolishing the father imago itself and, consequently, the collapse of the power of the phallus. The peril of this cataclysmic catastrophe is the castration threat, which I therefore specify as the *phallic castration threat.*

In formulating the phallic castration threat, I intend to convey that this threat pertains to the phantasmatic phallus, not the subjective sexual organ, the penis. The penis is only implicated in this context to the extent that it is identified with the phantasmatic phallus under the influence of the death drive. *The castration threat is an occurrence that unfolds on the level of unconscious structural phantasms.* It only seemingly has to do with subjective corporeality, and only insofar as the individual ego strives for an equation of penis and phallus.

The threat of castration prevents the appropriation of this protective phallus, making fusional incest with the mother impossible. As a result, the Oedipus complex becomes the complex of binding the death drive. This is its psychobiological meaning, which makes it, as said, after Freud´s formulation, not only the central core of all neuroses but of the psyche in general. The primal scene, therefore, is that psychic imagination in which the Natural Law relations are expressed which constitute and maintain the dimension of the psychical.

When the resolution of the conflict of the infantile depressive position is achieved by adopting the position outside, that is, through the inherently creative 'invention' of the position of the third and, by extension, of the father, the phallic threat of castration encompasses the resurgence of the conflict of the depressive position. The loss of the father imago revives the old good-bad split of the object and thus the paranoid attack on the life-sustaining object, which is hereby perceived as damaged and threatened in its existence. The subject, therefore, undergoes the experience of castration both on itself and on the object. In essence, it involves a regression to a structurally psychotic functional level. The collapse of the father imago represents the actual grandscale catastrophe of psychic life.

Because of this dynamic and structural meaning, the phallic threat of castration and behind it the threat of loss of the father imago becomes the agent of repression and in that way the agent of the creation of the *dynamically unconscious* part of the id. Here, repression uses the dimension of the structurally unconscious of the id, which has arisen in the transition from the splitting conception of the object to the reality-appropriate unified conception of it. Repression uses here the quality of the categorical unconsciousness of psychically nevertheless active contents, in order to establish a structurally secured non-identity of the contents to be repressed in relation to the ego of the position outside, i.e. a structurally secured non-fusion. This structural non-identity protects the ego of the position outside – the oedipal ego – from the danger of fusion, i.e. from the death drive. This is the purpose of repression.

The Female Oedipus Complex

These lines of thought prompt the question of the female Oedipus complex. The ego's desire for fusion with the primary object – expressed in oedipal terms as the yearning for fusional incest with the mother – would logically be regarded as an unconscious motive for both sexes. For the ego is an instance of the psychic apparatus and as such is not bound to gender. However, this perspective appears to be at odds with the prevailing heterosexual expression of female sexuality.

This contradiction is reconciled through the detour involving the psychic destiny of the child, a concept Freud articulated in 1933 in the "New Introductory Lectures on Psycho-Analysis." Freud stated: "The wish with which the girl turns to her father is no doubt originally the wish for the penis (...). The feminine situation is only established, however, if the wish for a penis is replaced by one for a baby, if, that is, a baby takes the place of a penis in accordance with an ancient symbolic equivalence" (p. 128).

With the aid of the – *phantasmatic* – child, which represents the paternal penis at the unconscious level of transference (the phallus received from the father and appropriated in the incestuous relationship to the father), the female ego aspires to enact the fusional incest with the mother. This is achieved by equating herself in her body with the mother from the primal scene and identifying in the ego with the phallic child. The identification of the ego with the phallus essentially signifies identification with the father from the primal scene. Consequently, it becomes a dramatization of the primal scene within the individual's own person.

Regarding the above emphasis on processes related to the phantasmatic child, it is important to clarify that we are discussing these matters at the level of cathexes and meanings within the framework of the unconscious structural phantasms. The unconscious oedipal phantasm pivots around this child. In the female psyche, the phantasm of the child with whom there is an incestuous relationship plays an unconsciously central structuring role, even if there is no actual child, and the notion of a real child doesn't prominently occupy the forefront of consciousness. This phantasm, on the part of the death drive, forms the background of desire which, if necessary, may lead to the manifestation of a real child.

One must not be misled by the concrete, apodictic-definitional assertiveness of these formulations. As stated, they relate to unconscious structural phantasms that never actually reach the surface of consciousness. They are, in essence, movements of the deep psyche. At this point, my aim is to describe the fundamental and, in this sense, essentially abstract structure of these phantasies, as they necessarily arise from the dynamics of the drives within the framework of oedipal phantasmatization. These are theoretical conclusions whose actual validity and concrete phantasmatic elaboration would need to be clarified by clinical research.

The specific castration threat of the female death drive would, therefore, be that the child's ego cannot assume this attribution as the paternal phallus due to its own fusional prohibition, which interlocks with that of the mother – essentially, due to its own castration threat. In other words, the child´s ego would collapse in an incestuous realization. This looming event of castration, stemming from the independent psychodynamics of the child, obstructs the fulfillment of the identificatory appropriation of the paternal phallus by the mother's ego and thereby preserves her position outside – the separation of ego and father imago.

The woman's bond with her own mother, which is in the background, is not merely a dormant latency but is the hidden primum movens also of heterosexual female sexual interest. In female sexuality as well, the desire for fusion of the ego with the primary object that fulfills all needs is the governing basic phantasy, which, on the unconscious level and from the perspective of the death drive, finds realization in orgasm. In any case, the appropriated paternal phallus is the key to that.

Biologically, one could argue that the purpose of this detour via the child is to ensure that the relationship to the child is an inherent part of the fundamental structural demands of the female psyche. Another conclusion drawn from this perspective is that, as a mother, the woman, through her incestuous renunciation towards the child, simultaneously safeguards the child itself from its own incestuous desires. By not seductively accommodating these desires, the mother helps create the necessary conditions for the fundamental developmental task imposed on the child's ego – namely, to renounce fusional incest.

On the level of the child's psychic reality, the emergence of the father imago and the stabilization of its function are dependent on the state of oedipal processing on the part of the mother. The mother allows and enables the child to build up the paternal phantasmatization or forbids it.

Sublimation

The concept of sublimation captures the pivotal insight derived from the theme of the structural binding of drive antagonism within the context of oedipal conflict dynamics. Specifically, sublimation becomes intelligible as the ego's self-abstention, optimally resulting from its confrontation with the oedipal conflict and the significance of the castration threat in relation to the temptation of incestuous corruption of the primal scene. This sublimative ego has learned that the castration threat does not target its own interests but rather preserves them by safeguarding the ego against the sole internal threat it faces – fusional incest. In sublimation, the ego recognizes the father imago as the operative imago, so to speak, of securing the ego, *representing the inherently anti-fusionary nature of the ego itself*. The father imago defines the nature of the ego as fundamentally non-identical to itself. As mentioned, this dynamic significance of the father imago is captured in the image of the primal scene, where the father unites with the mother without being lost in fusion, *embodying himself the anti-fusionary principle*.

When in the process of sublimation these levels of meaning of the primal scene imagination have been worked through by the ego and the ego has recognized the imperative of renouncing its desire to intrude and incestuously corrupt the primal scene, the primal scene can manifest in its true essence as the phantasmatic definition of the life drive, that is, safeguarding the ego against the danger of fusion with the representation of the object. In this context, the imago of the primal scene, from which the ego explicitly keeps itself out, is *the sublimative ego ideal*. This sublimative ego ideal signifies the culmination and completion of the structural development of the psyche, defining the nature of the ego – specifically, its antifusionary aspect – and thereby fortifying it against its endangerment from within itself.

The formation of the ego ideal involves the ultimate internalization of the relationship with the oedipal objects. At its core, the ego ideal comprises the imago of the primal scene, but in a version from which the ego has withdrawn – abandoning the incestuous demand. This abandonment is crucial for enabling internalization, as the desire for gratification by the real object has been relinquished. In other words, internalization becomes feasible only when the concrete desire for satisfaction, inherently tied to the real and external object, is renounced. This straightforward correlation holds significant central importance.

Thus, the fundamental development unfolds in a manner where, during the crisis of the infantile depressive position, the ego is separated from fusional desire. This desire is then conclusively prevented in the Oedipus complex by the threat of phallic castration. In the ego ideal, the ego recognizes these interconnections.

The circular processes of repeating, again and again, the themes and conflicts of the paranoid-schizoid and depressive positions echo throughout life the constitutive process of human psychic development: the separation of the ego from fusional desire by assuming the position outside, leading to the emergence of consciousness. This reflects the necessity to repeatedly acquire the quality of consciousness, as it is not an irreversible acquisition but a psychic function. It originates from a specific attitude of the ego where the ego distances itself from itself in a self-observing way and, consequently, undergoes a self-imposed splitting, rendering fusion impossible and thereby separating the ego from the object. The resultant quality of consciousness is essentially a by-product of this entire process and conflict, with the crucial aspect being the prevention of fusion due to the split in the ego.

The sublimative ego ideal, as the culmination of this entire development, is similarly not a fixed attainment but a potential structural trajectory that needs to be worked out again in each life conflict, to be imbued with vital truth. The sublimative ego ideal encapsulates the psychic meaning and significance of the process of mourning and renunciation of the illusion of omnipotent fusional control over the object. In exchange for control over the object, the ego gains its own security and stability as a structure, which intrapsychically can only be jeopardized by fusional desire.

This sublimatory movement represents the resolution of the oedipal conflict. Within it, the primary traumatization of the ego, stemming from the confrontation with the threat of its own annihilation as the consequence of its unavoidable desire for fusion, dissolves. In this manner, the traumatic nature of the ego would come to an end.

Annihilatory Aggression and Primary Envy

At the opposite end of the spectrum lies annihilatory aggression. The death drive's sexual trajectory aims to achieve, amid reality, a fusional unity with the primary object – meaning the object as such – by way of incest with the mother. This attempt fails because of the Oedipus complex and the threat of castration. The most extreme response to this encounter with the oedipal prohibition is the death drive, through annihilatory aggression, renouncing sexuality and the sexual oedipal project of fulfillment within reality and over the real object. Instead, it fundamentally assaults the real object, reality itself. The objective of this assault is to annihilate the real object, reverting to the imagination of the idealized object from the splitting constitution, and, beyond that, to the pre-ambivalent primary object of the pre-schizoid phase – the original promise of fulfillment of the death drive. The aim is to return to the stage of the 'subjective object,' predating the reality constitution of the object by the position outside and preceding the associated resolution of object splitting.

Therefore, this assault effectively aims at the revocation of the position outside, given that this position outside specifically paves the way for the apprehension of reality. Consequently, in targeting the real object, the death drive assaults the position outside and the father imago derived from it, the castration threat, and indeed the

Oedipus complex itself. Self-reflectivity and symbol formation are prerequisites for thinking at the level of the reality constitution of the ego. Consciousness is the functional and phenomenal outcome of the position outside. In this context, there exists a hatred of the dimension of consciousness itself, which, to eradicate consciousness, may extend to suicidal impulses. Suicidality and object aggression converge here. This is the background against which Bion (1970) writes in 'Attention and Interpretation` about hatred of reality and hatred of the cognitive functions enabling the perception of reality. It is about returning to the identity of the ego with the drive phantasm. Naturally, the assault on the reality dimension of the object also targets genital sexuality and gender difference, both intimately linked to the subject of reality.

In the subsequent stage of structural regression, the annihilatory death drive directs its assault toward the primal attachment of the primary object to psychosexuality, which forms *the foundation of attachment to the human object*, established in early orality during the initial days of life through the part object of the breast. For it is through this – from the point of view of the annihilatory death drive – 'error' of binding to the sexual object that the constitutive illusion of the Oedipus complex came about in the first place. In the course of annihilatory regression, the ego follows the attraction of the pre-schizoid phase, wherein the primary ego experienced a delusional sense of omnipotent fusional control over the still unsplit and, therefore, pre-ambivalent primary object – the representation of absolute abundance and completeness. With reference to this preambivalent object, an outside was not yet conceivable and, accordingly, the attachment to the sexual object, the breast, had not yet taken place. Hence, annihilatory aggression must target the attachment to the breast to revert to this preambivalent object.

Annihilatory aggression is therefore also directed against object constancy, that is, against the ability to compare one representation of the object with a previous one. The emergence of object constancy, after all, ends the pre-schizoid phase. In its assault on object constancy, annihilatory aggression is directed at memory, time and space – the fundamental components of object constancy. The ultimate objective is to achieve unity with the preambivalent object.

We are dealing here with the motor of that fanatical destruction which is directed against every form of human bond: from rampage to genocide and from neglect to suicide. Janine Chasseguet-Smirgel (2003) has described this psychic constellation in her work on the public hara-kiri suicide of the Japanese poet Yukio Mishima.

The pivotal point is that annihilatory aggression relates entirely to the realm of *internal object constitution,* progressing through the stages of object constancy, paranoid object splitting, depressive position, and position outside, attempting to forcefully reverse this process. Thus, annihilatory aggression appears to be aimed at the external object, but, in reality, it targets *the internal prerequisites for perceiving the external object.* Annihilatory aggression, fully correctly, identifies the external object with the Oedipus complex and sexuality.

Annihilatory aggression attempts to enforce regression across the entire course of ontogenesis of object representation, that is, of object constitution.

These reflections on annihilatory aggression have obvious implications for the metapsychology of primary encapsulated autism, which plays such a significant role in the ideas presented here, as it establishes the clinical necessity of a new psychoanalytic metapsychology[1]: From two perspectives, it is tempting to view

---

1 I would like to thank my wife Heike Zagermann for pointing out this link.

primary encapsulated autism as a manifestation of annihilatory aggression. Clinically, it is characterized by a developmental fixation occurring before primal attachment is acquired, resulting in a loss of the capacity to relate. Metapsychologically, it involves the foreclosure of object representation, as the object is experienced as the withdrawing not-me object. Thus, encapsulated autism entails a fully developed pathognomonic regression to an exclusive relationship with the purely intrapsychic primary object of the pre-schizoid phase before the manifestation of the not-me object.

I have already outlined above that the not-me object arises through the traumatic onset of fusional fear when approaching a fusional realization. This fusional fear is experienced as a rejection of the ego's claim to omnipotent control over the object, leading to the transformation of the object representation into the not-me object – a representation of the object that evades the omnipotence claim of the ego. As a consequence of this experienced rejection, the not-me object is foreclosed; that is, the psychic relations to this not-me object are severed. Since this process occurs under the conditions of totality and globality of the pre-schizoid phase, this signifies the complete collapse of the object relationship. It results in a regression to the illusory relationship with the primordial object of abundance and completeness – i.e., before the manifestation of the not-me object –, which seemingly does not evade the fusional claim.

Encapsulated autism indeed represents the genetically earliest case of annihilatory aggression and regression. To put it succinctly: *The foreclosure of the not-me object is an annihilatory aggression.* It's crucial to emphasize that the central pathodynamic element is the ego's unconditional claim to omnipotence, that is, the absolute demand for omnipotent control over the object. It cannot be overstated that the absolute and, in a sense, brutal theme of omnipotence is the distinguishing characteristic of the ego in the pre-schizoid phase. The experienced ruthlessness of the not-me object is merely a reflection of the brutality of this omnipotence.

Evidently, the key concept in this discussion of annihilatory aggression is primary envy, as described by Melanie Klein in 1957. Klein views this envy as the fundamental destructive force, aimed at the goodness of the good object, when the object eludes the subject's omnipotent control. Envy thus serves as the complementary opposite to the death drive's fusional impulse. It is activated when this impulse meets substantial resistance in realizing its phantasies. Envy poses a significant threat to the ego, endangering both its internal and external objects.

Primary envy is distinct from annihilatory aggression as just described. It emerges from an ego despairing at its inability to incorporate the object into its egocentric omnipotence. This despair leads to a furious campaign of annihilation against the withdrawing object. This is primary envy. It represents a death drive frustrated in achieving its goal, making it the fundamentally suicidal force. Primary envy is instrumental in the foreclosure of the primary object – the not-me object – in cases of psychogenic encapsulation autism, as it embodies the earliest form of aggression. This aggression is in response to the object's self-withdrawal as the primary expression of the antifusionary principle of the life drive. Frances Tustin (1972, 1981), in her autism theory, refers to this withdrawing object as the 'not-me object'.

Annihilatory aggression and primary envy exist on a continuum of destructive regression. Annihilatory aggression can evolve into primary envy when, in the course of structural regression, it faces the realization that fusion is unattainable, even when reality, position outside, and object constancy are suspended. Both primary envy and annihilatory aggression draw their force and dangerousness from their origin in the pre-schizoid phase, characterized by its attributes of globality, totality, and timelessness.

These reflections on the origin of primary envy and annihilatory aggression suggest that aggression, even at its most fundamental level, should not be viewed as an autonomous drive. Instead, it represents one of the potential complications in the ego's interaction with the death drive. In this respect, it is fundamentally not different from those particular maladjustments of the ego that give rise to the major nosological categories.

Object constancy and the autistic hole

Let me reiterate the points previously expounded regarding object constancy: Object constancy is the ability, maturing neuronally over time, to maintain the object representation constant in time beyond the moment of the stimulus presentation that evokes it, hence the term object constancy. It establishes the capacity *to compare* a current object representation with a preceding one. Thus, the focus is on comparing object representations over time, introducing the epistemic concept of time into mental experience. Simultaneously, the temporal succession of object representations initiates the conceptualization of space as the third dimension, with the initial experience of space arising from the successive representations of the object. Consequently, space becomes the second fundamental epistemic category, complementing time. This developmental transition marks the conclusion of the pre-schizoid phase, characterized by a total and global – i.e., non-comparable – experience of the object that takes place in timelessness.

It is crucial to recognize that, in this context, we are confronting a fundamentally distinct concept of the object during the pre-schizoid phase. We are not dealing with the Freudian or Kleinian object, both of which have spatial and temporal localization. Instead, we encounter an object conception situated in an asymbolic and non-dimensional realm of experience. From the standpoint of conscious experience, this mode of existence remains inaccessible directly. It can only be apprehended through imagination, in a more or less abstract manner. Put differently, this experience, detached from space and time, is inherently unconscious, lacking the intrinsic capacity for consciousness.

In the evolution of psychoanalytic theory, the location of the pre-schizoid phase in an inaccessible dimension devoid of space and time has led to the assumption of an initial stage characterized by the merging of self and object representation – an era marked by fusion and absolute dependence, as the starting point of psychic ontogenesis. This perspective equated the absence of space and time with a fusional state, a misconception carrying profound implications for our understanding of human development. Contrary to this belief, spacelessness and timelessness in the pre-schizoid phase are not indicative of a fusional state but rather the outcome of yet-to-be-achieved object constancy. Fundamentally, the preschizoid phase represents a neurologically determined state.

The challenge in tolerating separateness does not stem from a lingering residue of primary fusion that, as per the conventional perspective, must be gradually transcended. Instead, it arises from the influence of the death drive, which persistently seeks to actualize the fusion of ego and object representation throughout one's life. Initially, it is not an encounter with boundless fusional dependence, but rather an experience of the absolute omnipotence of the ego confronted with an object of absolute completeness.

The crucial line of reasoning is that, with the transition to object constancy, *the material object becomes apprehensible as a spatial body*, as the material, corporeal, bodily object can only be grasped through its being situated in space and time. The material object, defined within the dimensions of space and time, is associated with the possibility of establishing *a relationship with the object as another body*. The immaterial primary object of the pre-schizoid phase transforms into the object as a body that can be related to. This marks the pivotal moment where *the notion of the other body becomes conceivable*, subsequently giving rise, through primary identification, to the idea of another ego residing within that body. Additionally, with the capacity for comparison and alternative, object constancy inherently includes the ability to conceptualize and form relationships with a variety of bodies.

These considerations become practically relevant as the capacity to grasp space and time – object constancy – and consequently, the ability to conceive of bodies, is linked to the capability to establish contact with the specifically material, bodily breast located exclusively in space and time, and thereby, *primal attachment*. Without object constancy, lacking space and time, no connection with the breast can be forged. This implies that attachment to the human object, the human other, fails to materialize. This scenario unfolds in primary encapsulated autism and manifests as a clinical reality. Space and time are not inherent aspects of human perception; rather, they are acquired. Conversely, this signifies that perception exists before space and time – the pre-schizoid phase. Space and time serve not only as categories of our epistemic cognition and the coordinate system of the material world but are primarily prerequisites for its very concrete accessibility and the capacity to establish relationships – especially relationships with other bodies.

As outlined, the foreclosure of the not-me object in primary encapsulated autism requires the state of globality and totality characteristic of the pre-schizoid phase, as well as a condition preceding object constancy, where the object representation has not yet been split according to the good-bad dichotomy. Only under these conditions is the total and global foreclosure of the object conceivable. It is crucial to realize that under the conditions of totality and globality characteristic of the pre-schizoid phase, the foreclosure of the not-me object does not merely imply the foreclosure of this specific representation of the object opposing fusion but signifies the wholesale foreclosure of the object representation as such. This underscores the catastrophic nature of this process.

The material world is the domain where relationships unfold and become possible – initially with partial objects, later with whole objects, but in any case, with bodies, even if imaginary. Object constancy is the gateway to this material world. Thus, it is object constancy that demarcates the pre-schizoid phase from the subsequent stages of development. If object constancy fails to materialize due to the pre-schizoid foreclosure of the primary object (because there are no meaningful representations left for object constancy to work with), it implies that a connection to the spatiotemporal, bodily object of the material world cannot be established. Primal attachment to the breast fails to materialize. The child remains confined within the realm of pre-schizoid object relationships, leading to the development of primary encapsulated autism.

This situation accounts for the extremely early onset of primary autistic encapsulation disorder. Frances Tustin posits its occurrence in the first days of life, potentially interpartum or even intrauterine, *explicitly preceding the time of primal attachment.* As elucidated, object constancy is the precondition for localizing the object as a body in space and time – a necessity for the primal attachment of the object representation to the partial object of the breast. Establishing a relationship with the breast, as a process in the material world, demands access to space and time because, without these, the breast – conceived as a body – cannot be located and retrieved. *Hence, without object constancy, attachment becomes unattainable.*

Therefore, the fixation point of primary encapsulated autism is situated before object constancy and thus before primal attachment. This is the correlation highlighted by Frances Tustin, emphasizing the absence of primal attachment in children with primary autistic encapsulation.

It is essential to recognize that object constancy, by facilitating access to space and time and, consequently, the apprehension of bodies, introduces a fundamentally new element into the psyche – the theme of separation, inherently tied to bodies by their very separateness. In essence, this represents a traumatic experience *for everyone*, and all subsequent psychological development can be framed as a process of coping with this experience, for the separation of bodies naturally stands in stark contradiction to the fusional intent of the death drive. Thus, it must also be stated that primal attachment only unfolds its significance insofar as it is connected to the inner perception of the other – i.e., separated – body. A preference for the breast without simultaneous acceptance of the other body (as with Tustin's little patient John, who will be discussed later) does not constitute a primal attachment. For the rest, the traumatic not-me object of primary autistic development is not a manifestation of separation but rather a collapse of the omnipotence demand of the pre-schizoid ego.

To comprehend this interrelation more precisely, it is crucial to keep in mind that the pre-schizoid world is a realm of absolute presentness and availability. In this world, the total and global primary object represents completeness and abundance, confronting an ego that perceives itself as omnipotent. In any case, and this is the crucial point, there is no representation or experience of separation in this early pre-schizoid world. While there is a prohibition of fusion, there is no separation. Separation only becomes relevant with bodies, signifying: with object constancy.

It should be noted that this breakthrough associated with object constancy, leading to the perception of the other body and the primal attachment of object representation to the other body – the breast –, lays the foundation for the oedipal sexual phantasmatisation. From this point forward, the death drive must seek a way to fulfill its fusional phantasy within the context of relationships with other bodies that are bodily separated from each other as well as from the ego/subject. This difficulty that arises with bodies is the primary catalyst for the annihilatory aggression that seeks to dissolve the bodies and the separation inherent in them. The goal is to return to the state of the pre-schizoid phase with its promise of fusional fulfillment, the ego's omnipotence, and the object's abundance and completeness.

In the pre-schizoid phase, we navigate a dimension of psychic experience that essentially is a different dimension: outside of space and time. To say it again, it appears crucial to acknowledge that this representation of the object defies conscious imagination entirely. An experience beyond the constraints of space and time eludes our intuition and empathy, inherently tied to space and time. This is why primary autistic children, residing in this spaceless and timeless dimension, seem so isolated and cut off. We can only try to draw them out by connecting to the purely sensorial qualities of the pre-schizoid phase. The criteria of movement, connectivity, receptivity, and reciprocity, as highlighted by Joshua Durban and others in the evaluation and treatment of primary autistic children, for this reason also originate from the pre-schizoid sensorial realm.

Once the child genuinely attempts to move out of this pre-schizoid world, they are internally confronted with the absence of primal attachment. This marks the onset of the anxieties of being (Durban 2014), where the catastrophe of unattachment unfolds: to dissolve, to liquefy, to leak, to fall to pieces, to fall forever, to have no skin or a skin full of holes, to be literally skinned, to burn, to freeze, to suffocate, to lose the sense of time and space and all orientation, to lose part or parts of the body. In the background, as an escalated stage, are the diffuse-osmotic anxieties (Durban 2021), representing an even more archaic form of anxiety where the toxic attack is felt to come from everywhere and nowhere. From my point of view, these diffuse-osmotic anxieties manifest the dimensionlessness of the pre-schizoid phase, hence the sense that the attack originates from everywhere and nowhere.

The anxieties of being and the diffuse-osmotic anxieties are the symptoms of the failure of primal attachment and, thus, the failure of attachment to space and time. However, their emergence signals the child's attempt to move out of the primary autistic encapsulation. These anxieties indicate the distress (Leidensdruck) stemming from the awareness of the missing primal attachment and, beyond that, access to space and time, the other body. The existential threat posed by these fears is rooted in the inability to access space and time: to fall forever, to dissolve, to lose the sense of all orientation, and so forth.

Above all, the primary autistic blockade of object constancy, as previously outlined, impacts the primal attachment to the breast, obstructing its establishment. The autistic hole, serving as the indication of the absent cathexis of the breast defined in space and time – that is, the object associated with established object constancy – becomes the signifier of a developmental process that has not unfolded. This developmental default manifests itself in the experience of a hole.

For readers less acquainted with the features of primary encapsulated autism: The autistic hole is a clinical manifestation observed in primary encapsulated autists who experience a hole on the front of their body, typically in the abdominal region, in the sense of a very specific, real defect and a traumatic lack of protection. This experience leads them to seek compensation through the use of an autistic object. This autistic object is often hard and angular, tightly grasped in their hand, as an attempt to transfer the perception of hardness as a protective armor or shield to the autistic hole.

If we connect the autistic hole with the failure of object constancy, it signifies how much the experience of space and time, the connection to the bodily object – specifically, the breast –, and primal attachment is inherent to the constitution of the human psyche. The failure of this experience presents itself as a hole.

The autistic hole also serves as the representation of the foreclosure of the not-me object from the pre-schizoid phase. As detailed previously, this foreclosure, under the condition of globality and totality of the pre-schizoid phase, acquires the comprehensive meaning of a complete foreclosure of the representation of the primary object as such. This global traumatization – as the experience of an elemental lack – is expressed in the hole. Tustin, therefore, has seen the hole as the expression of a lesion, indicating quite concretely the loss, the foreclosure of the object.

The driving force behind the foreclosure of the not-me object is the powerful attraction of the world of the primordial pre-schizoid phase. *The object representation of the primordial pre-schizoid phase before the manifestation of the not-me object remains intact.* In this world, there exists an object representation characterized by absolute, present completeness and abundance, coupled with an ego possessing absolute omnipotence. It is a realm devoid of separation, the latter being connected to the world of spatiotemporal bodies and object constancy. The absence of separation constitutes the attracting force propelling annihilatory aggression and annihilatory regression. This attraction stands as the genetic precipitating factor for the manifestation of primary encapsulated autism.

In this context, I want to emphasize my foundational hypothesis that the psychical emerges from perception, specifically the confrontation of the ego with the object during the act of perception. Based on this hypothesis, it logically follows that the object cannot be fundamentally foreclosed as long as psychic life exists.

Given the premise of these considerations, the autistic hole assumes a propulsive meaning. As explained, it contains the awareness not only of the lesion connected to the foreclosure of the not-me object, but of the inhibition of a destined and necessary developmental progression. Consequently, efforts should be made to discourage autistic children from disavowing the autistic hole through reliance on the autistic object. *The gateway to development is found within the autistic hole.*

To summarize the entire developmental process: Object constancy enables the apprehension of three-dimensional bodies in space and time, forming relationships with them. This serves as the prerequisite for establishing primal attachment. In primary identification, these bodies are endowed with an own ego, just as the subject perceives itself within primary identification as an explicit ego. As the oedipal development unfolds, the potential for relationships between these bodies – or other selves, other egos – becomes conceivable. This introduces the challenge of excluding the ego from the interactions of others, as one can oneself exclude the third party within the relationship to the second. However, in the absence of object constancy, the ego remains confined within the dimensionless, asymbolic, sensory realm of the pre-schizoid phase, with a total and global object representation that appears to be of absolute completeness, coupled with an ego of omnipotence as the governing principle. Yet, this state lacks access to the spatiotemporal, bodily object of the material world and, consequently, to the other ego. This is the condition of primary autistic encapsulation.

The formation of primal attachment – the initial bond with a human counterpart – is a reversible process, as annihilatory aggression shows. In the realm of basic infantile experience, the counterbalance to this annihilatory regression is the love of the breast; that is, the love emanating from both psychologically and physically nourishing relational experiences. I interpret this quite literally: the force that upholds this primal attachment is the satisfaction experienced in the relationship, both physically and psychologically. This is why Freud was so right in placing sexuality at the very center of his focus: sexuality is essentially the paraphrase of this connection. Conversely, this implies that the risk of annihilatory regression emerges when basic needs are not satisfied for an extended duration. However, this perspective is complicated by the fact that such unmet needs may not always be objective but can stem from subjective, defense-related obstructions.

The Pathologies

The categories of pathology are then defined by the varying degrees and types of the ego's opposition to the threat of castration and the

66

prohibition of fusion. To some extent, for psychosis and borderline pathology, I have already outlined this above.

On the neurotic structural level, the ego reluctantly submits to the threat of castration but does not internally accept its implications. This results in the ongoing loss of further personality aspects through repression. Anything associated with the fusional context becomes unconscious, thereby ensuring *the ego's non-identity with the subject matter endangered by fusion*. This process constitutes the dynamic unconscious. The triadic pattern of denial, which is a hallmark of hysteria as the most structurally advanced form of neurotic disorder, can be seen as a paradigm for the entire range of neurotic symptoms. This triad includes the denial of castration threat, the denial of sex difference, and the denial of reflective consciousness.

Precisely, neurotic pathology is situated on the structural level of the position of the ego outside the drive phantasm. This level is characterized by the ego's access to reality and the father imago being in function, aligning it with the oedipal structural level. In this context, the predominant anxiety experienced is castration anxiety.

In the perverse personality organization, the pathognomonic splitting of the phallus from the father imago, as described by Joyce McDougall in 1972, results in a scenario where the father imago is devalued and foreclosed as the fictive originator of incest prohibition and castration threat. However, the phallic imago remains excessively idealized. The phallic castration threat continues to be active in terms of the prohibition of identity of ego and phallus. The attempt to transgress this prohibition leads to the intense near-psychotic panic attacks characteristic of the perverse organization. Thus, even though the father imago is devalued in the perverse structure, the nonidentity of ego and phallus – and therefore the paternal principle – persists. Consequently, the perverse personality organization signifies a structurally relatively stable intermediate stage in the progression of structural regression that leads to psychic pathology.

As this aspect is crucial for the discussion to follow, I revisit the psychodynamics of the father imago and the imago of the phallus. I have previously explained that the ego's position outside the drive phantasm, or in short the position outside, resolves the crisis of the depressive position. This resolution involves a self-reflective splitting of the ego within itself, enabling the ego to become the object of its own reflection. This signifies the overcoming of the good-bad split in object representation as mode of defense against the fusional death drive. The split within the ego now serves this defensive purpose because the totality demanded by the death drive's fusional desire is incompatible with a split ego — a part of the ego would always remain external to the fusion. This overcoming of the good-bad split of the object is synonymous with gaining access to reality, as reality necessitates a unified, not split, representation of the object.

The position outside thus serves as the gateway to reality, self-reflective consciousness, and the formation of symbols, and consequently to all higher functions of the psyche. To structurally consolidate and protect this position, it finds personal expression in the father imago. This father imago represents the self-reflective non-identity of the ego with itself, embodying the position outside. It implies an absolute prohibition against the ego identifying with the father, a prohibition that is unconditional. This is because the identity of ego and father would negate the essence of the father imago, which lies in the personification of the ego's non-identity with itself. This dynamic sets the stage for the oedipal conflict, where the father appears to engage in sexual activity with the mother with impunity – i.e. without dissolving –, as this is an act the ego that is under the influence of the death drive, interprets in a fusional manner. In truth, though, the father, although disavowed by the oedipal ego, embodies the antifusionary principle, implying and reinforcing the ego's non-identity with itself.

However, as previously mentioned, the ego, on a superficial level, remains unaware of the profound significance of the father – or more precisely, the ego influenced by the death drive disregards this significance – leading the oedipal ego to attempt to usurp the father's capacity for fusional incest with the mother. From the perspective of the oedipal ego, which by this time has undergone infantile psychosexual development, the father's power, serving as a safeguard against the fusional threat of ego dissolution, is epitomized in the imago of the phallus. This imago represents the tool, the instrument through which the father unites with the mother. Against this backdrop, perverse structure formation results in the phallus being split off from the father imago and leads to the devaluation and foreclosure of the father, insofar as he embodies the incest prohibition. This prohibition is thus interpreted as the father's assertion of possession and exclusive rights over the phallus. Consequently, the perverse splitting off of the phallus from the father imago *directly challenges the incest prohibition.*

Yet, the perverse ego discovers that the endeavor to claim the phallus for itself, that is, to achieve identity between ego and phallus, remains futile. This is because the phallus, as representation of the paternal principle, inherently upholds and contains the prohibition against identifying with the ego. In essence, the moment the ego attempts to equate itself with the phallus, the phallus ceases to serve its protective role. This is the threat of phallic castration that the perverse ego faces, even after the perishing of the father imago.

This explanation of the background dynamics leads by itself to an understanding of perverse symptomatology. One must assume that the perverse structure is comprised of two distinct functional realms.

In the first realm, associated with the devalued and foreclosed father imago, the ego is compelled to revert to splitting the object into good and bad as the mode of defense against the death drive. This regression results from the loss of the position outside due to the foreclosure of the father imago. Consequently, the ego forfeits its capacity for self-reflection, symbol formation, and access to reality. In other words, within this domain, the ego functions psychotically. In contrast, within the second realm, concerning the ego's relationship to the usurped, pirated and appropriated phallus, the threat of castration remains operative. As a result, the ego of necessity remains in the reflective distancing from itself; it is within this sphere that access to reality and symbolic function are preserved. The ego functions non-psychotically.

Thus, the defining feature of perverse structure formation is the *simultaneous* psychotic and non-psychotic functioning of the ego. One area of personality is governed by the oedipal triangulation of ego, object, and phallus. In contrast, within the other area, the disintegration of the father imago leads to the loss of the position outside and consequently, access to reality. This results in the reemergence of the early, pre-oedipal triangulation involving the ego and the good and bad split objects. Psychosis and non-psychosis coexist.

In this manner, the paradoxical coexistence of denying and acknowledging reality, as well as denying and acknowledging separation from the object in the midst of reality – a hallmark of the perverse structure – emerges. John Steiner (1993) termed this phenomenon "narcissistic perversion" to highlight its broader relevance for personality diagnosis, distinct from the notion of sexual perversion. This split in perceiving reality carries profound destructive and corrupting implications across all contexts of object relations and, consequently, social interaction.

Janine Chasseguet-Smirgel's (1975 and passim) conceptualization of perversion as an abbreviation of the long path of oedipal conflict and controversy, via the fabrication of an artificial, inauthentic phallus – a "faux semblant" – aligns conceptually with these insights. This notion suggests that perversion serves as a bypass to the complex and challenging resolution of oedipal tensions, opting instead for the creation – fabrication – of a false symbol of potency and completeness.

Thus, the splitting-off of the phallus from the father imago implies a splitting of the ego into two domains: one where the father is devalued and foreclosed, and another where the paternal role is active and authoritative, particularly in maintaining the threat of castration in relation to the phallus. This perverse splitting of the ego is structurally stable and robust, illustrating a deep-seated division, a split in how authority and power are internalized and contested within the psyche.

The borderline constitution, on one hand, fundamentally also involves the splitting-off of the idealized phallus from the devalued father imago and the attempt to claim this idealized phallus for oneself. As such, the borderline constitution represents a manifestation of perverse structural formation, marking a significant preliminary conclusion. However, distinct from the general perverse structure, the defining feature of the borderline organization is the explicit and central battle against the threat of castration. Structurally, unlike in the general perverse structure, there is no stable ego split here like that between the domain of the devalued father imago and that of the idealized phallus. For example, as a split between acknowledging the castration threat in one realm but not in the other. *The borderline constitution does not acknowledge the castration threat in any case.* Instead, the guiding principle of the borderline constitution is an outright rebellion against the castration threat.

The ego splitting in this context emerges as a dynamic, fluctuating process, contingent on the ego's oscillating resistance to the castration threat – sometimes acknowledging its defeat, and at other times, launching into a renewed, fierce counterattack. The critical factor is not the fundamental acknowledgment or denial of the castration threat – such acknowledgment is, in fact, not even on the table. Instead, the issue is structurally simpler: whether the ego, in any given moment, is distancing itself from the phallus under pressure or actively attacking this distancing. Thus, the borderline condition manifests as highly unstable, volatile and, to an external observer, seemingly unpredictable, vacillating between periods of purely psychotic functioning and others resembling a quasi-neurotic operational level. Nevertheless, underlying all this, as previously mentioned, is the perverse splitting-off of the phallus from the father imago.

Narcissistic perversion, defined as the simultaneous denial and acknowledgment of both reality and separation from the object, serves as the pathological foundation for both the general perverse personality organization and borderline disorders. This general perverse organization as well as the borderline condition revolve around the psychic representation of the omnipotent, magical, narcissistic phallus and its acquisition, with this phallus being dissociated from the devalued and foreclosed paternal imago. *This constitutes the perverse dynamic.* Consequently, the perverse dynamic emerges as a far more extensive basic motif of psychopathology than previously recognized.

In summary, the core idea represents a significant broadening of the concept of perversion: perversion, as a nosological category, encompasses all clinical manifestations that originate from the splitting off of the idealized phallus from the devalued paternal imago. Specifically, this indicates that borderline disorders are fundamentally to be considered as perverse manifestations. Within the spectrum of perverse disorders, borderline pathology stands out as the most structurally advanced, yet undeniably embodying a perverse dynamic.

On the other hand, the fundamental distinction between the neurotic and the perverse structure lies in the fact that, in neurosis, there is no splitting off of the phallus from the paternal imago. As a result, the threat of castration is not simultaneously acknowledged and denied. Because of this, the unmitigated threat of castration causes repression.

Thus, there are four main territories of psychopathology:

1. disorders at the level of the pre-schizoid phase: the autistic diseases;
2. psychotic disorders: the position outside is not established, the ego functions in identity with the drive phantasm and consequently there is a good-bad split of object representation. Access to reality is not given;
3. the structurally perverse disorders: it is about the theft, the appropriation of the phallus, the phallus is split off from the father imago, which in turn is devalued. On the perverse structural level there is accordingly a mixture of oedipal contents and dynamics and, on the other hand, themes based on the good-bad dichotomy, that is, the splitting of the object;
4. the neurotic level, in which the castration threat is unrestrictedly valid, and the disturbance is purely oedipal in nature.

Regarding homosexualities, to the extent that they are considered within the context of psychopathology – that is, within the framework of drive-defense dynamics – female homosexuality emerges from the devaluation of the father and the splitting off of the phallus from the paternal imago, akin to what is observed in the perverse structural disposition. This devaluation prevents the development of the phantasy, seen in normal female psychodynamics, of conceiving the phallic child with the father. Consequently, one's own body is wholly equated with the phallus, and the mother is identified with the partner. This scenario pertains to the realm of the basic, deeply unconscious structural phantasms, regardless of how roles are distributed in the actual sexual relationship, which evolves from the complex interplay of mutual projections and identifications.

Joyce McDougall (1978) has compellingly detailed how panic attacks in female homosexuality are linked to the issue of separation, whether temporary or permanent. Separation represents the specific form of castration threat here, since in separation, due to the manifestation of deficiency, the experience of loss triggers a fusional phantasy, leading to the breakdown of the protective phallic phantasmatization. In the absence of separation, the urge towards this fusional phantasy is kept at bay by the compulsion to constantly maintain intense, concrete bodily closeness – a trait notably characteristic of female homosexual relationships. The purpose of this bodily closeness is to minimize frustration and, consequently, the urge for fusion, as the devaluation of the father imago complicates the blocking of fusional phantasies through a fully realized oedipal primal scene phantasmatization.

Male homosexuality, accordingly, centers on the acquisition of the magical, omnipotent phallus that has been dissociated, split off from the paternal imago. Towards this phallus, a range of attitudes can be taken, from manic identification to adopting a feminine-receptive stance. However, the sexual engagement with a woman – unconsciously the mother as the original object of fusion – is considered too dangerous, because here the phallic castration threat manifests itself. It should be noted that in male homosexuality, the phantasy of fusion and consequently castration – that is, the impotence of the protective phallus – is perpetually imminent, making phallic reassurance particularly crucial.

Both female and male homosexuality, insofar as they are considered psychopathologies, stem from the pathognomonic splitting off of the idealized phallus from the devalued paternal imago. Thus, structurally seen, it is basically a matter of a psychic functioning according to a perverse organization or – depending on the extent of denial of castration thread – a borderline organization.

If the battle against separation from the object, driven by the death drive, is seen as the underlying motive for all psychopathological manifestations, it simultaneously implies that this motive – characterized by the striving for coincidence of ego and object representation – should be equated with the narcissistic striving. Consequently, narcissism emerges as the ubiquitous element across all forms of psychic pathology, a concept already articulated by Rosenfeld in 1964. *Therefore, narcissism and the death drive are to be considered synonymous and identical.*

It was also Rosenfeld who, in his seminal 1971 study on the aggressive aspects of narcissism, demonstrated that narcissism is consistently linked with aggression. If the death drive and narcissism coincide, this connection with aggression is clarified by the nature of the death drive to ruthlessly utilize the object as a means of satisfaction – essentially, as a means, as tool to eliminate deficiency or lack. All psychic behaviors and tendencies that treat the object as an exploitable resource can be attributed to the death drive. The death drive disregards the object's autonomy, devaluing and effectively extinguishing it, which explains the narcissistic individual's seeming indifference towards the independent object.

This further implies that the destructive-exploitative components of the ego, under the sway of the death drive, are idealized, as described by Rosenfeld. He elucidated this through the concept of the pathological narcissistic organization, where those destructive, split off components of the ego, organized as a mafia-like entity, strive to dominate and subjugate the object and those facets of the ego associated with the life drive.

In this understanding, aggression and the death drive are associated, yet aggression is not the primary driving force, the primum movens of the death drive as it was for Freud; rather, it serves as one of its instruments. This association is linked to the theme of exerting control over the object.

Psychopathology, therefore, should be understood in terms of the various strategies by which an ego, under the influence of the death drive, seeks to assert control over the object, aiming to thus eliminate the separation between ego and object. Underpinning this endeavor is the phantasy of fusion with the object.

Projective Identification

At the most primitive level, when the fusional intention is not sought through an omnipotent global introjection of the object, the primary operational mechanism of the death drive – which reflects the narcissistic quest for coincidence of ego and object representation – is omnipotent projective identification. The objective of projective identification is to erase the distinction between ego and object. This mechanism pursues its goal by projecting undesirable aspects of the ego onto the object, all the while retaining control over them. This process, in terms of both the act of projection and the aspect of control, aims to undermine and, fundamentally, eliminate the separation between ego and object.

One must understand this against the background of the constitutive fusional phantasy of the pre-schizoid phase. The idea of fusion is born in the pre-schizoid phase from the act of perception, that is, as a consequence of the structure of perception, which is composed of the perceiving ego and the perceived object. In the pre-schizoid phase, the ego attempts to compensate for its own experienced deficiency by way of fusion with the primary object. The projection of the aversive contents into the object is the first step in this process. That this step is within the framework of a global fusion movement is proven by the following moment of the maintained control of the ego over the projected aversive contents, insofar as this control is explained by the fusional theme standing in the background. Fusion is the maximum control.

Projective identification can be fully understood theoretically only when considered in the context of the pre-schizoid phase, as the fusional theme inherent to this phase elucidates the simultaneous occurrence of projection and control. The descent of projective identification from the pre-schizoid phase is further evidenced by the fact that it is not based on splitting, but on a global fusional intention. This is only compatible with the still unsplit object of the pre-schizoid phase. The archaic nature of projective identification is indisputable. It cannot relate to the unsplit object of the neurotic functional level. Thus, projective identification originates in the pre-schizoid phase and is the agent and vehicle of the pre-schizoid fusional movement. Since the primary object of the pre-schizoid phase is the sum total of all that is good and the omnipotent means of abolishing lack, the object is not affected and compromised by the projection of the aversive content. Instead, the object is trusted and anticipated to neutralize the deficiency.

Frances Tustin also observed a connection between projective identification and the earliest mental states. Suzanne Maiello (1997, p. 10) references a 1982 letter from Tustin, stating: "(...) my notion of the predecessor to 'projective identification' being 'flowing-over-at-oneness'". She further explains elsewhere: "'Flowing-over-at-oneness' is the process by which the illusion of 'primal unity' is maintained" (1981, p. 80). Tustin thus makes an explicit connection between fusional striving and projective identification.

Projective identification is thus associated with the pre-schizoid phase via the global fusional theme, and therefore with its notions of omnipotence, totality and globality, and timelessness. This accounts for the quasi-absolute power and force of projective identification as well as for its essentially unconscious mode of operation. The pre-schizoid phase is essentially unconscious because, due to the absence of developed object constancy, the ego cannot achieve any comparative distance from the experience of the immediate moment.

The concept of projective identification was first introduced by Melanie Klein in 1946. She regarded projective identification as the main mechanism of defense against the process of mourning, crucial for resolving the conflict of the depressive position. In my view, this mourning refers not only to the damage done to the good object but, more significantly, to the acknowledgement of separateness between ego and object, which emerges as the structural result of the conflict of the depressive position. Insofar as projective identification inherently negates this separation by its very nature, it is in fact the mechanism of defense against mourning over this separation.

Projective identification, along with her delineation of the paranoid-schizoid and depressive positions, stands as Melanie Klein's seminal contribution to psychoanalytic theory. I have previously discussed how projective identification pertains to the structural relationships and dynamics characteristic of the pre-schizoid phase, suggesting that a comprehensive theoretical explanation of projective identification necessitates understanding it within this context. Given that Melanie Klein is closely associated with the discovery of the paranoid-schizoid and depressive positions – representing a world marked by the good-bad split of the object – it can be argued that with her theory of projective identification, she, in a manner of speaking, transcended her own foundational concepts. By implicitly acknowledging the existence of a pre-schizoid phase through projective identification, Klein expanded the scope of her theoretical framework beyond its original boundaries.

Within the framework of Bion's (1962a, 1962b) concept of the alpha function, however, projective identification acquires an entirely different significance. It becomes a fundamental means and medium of communication between mother and child, insofar as the mother absorbs her child's projective identifications into her to comprehend the child's psychic states, metabolizes them psychically, and then returns them to the child in a "digested" form, also through projective identification. This understanding lays the groundwork for the field theory of the analytic relationship. I view this dynamic as a quintessential example of a life drive-related inversion of a death drive psychic relationship. Such inversions are integral to the entire process of psychic development and structure formation, resulting from the antagonism between the drives. The Oedipus complex is the most notable instance, embodying both life drive and death drive dimensions of meaning.

Summary

To summarize, the basic train of thought is that the psychical, including its drives, develops out of itself without precondition and is constituted on the basis of the perceptual function from the relation of ego and object. The drives arise from this relationship and manifest its inherent conflicts. Psychic structure formation is the consequence of the confrontation with this conflictuality and its internal lawful order.

The most significant insights from my analysis include:

1. The system psyche is based on representations. These representations act as a screen or membrane, separating the psyche from the soma. Only those elements that undergo the process of becoming inscribed as representations can be considered psychic content. Thus, even information that might be encoded in the systemic properties of other brain parts must first initiate a representation formation process for its activation at the cortical level. This applies to a range of concepts, including Panksepp's basic emotions, Solms' neurobiological drives, or developmental psychological insights such as those of Piaget or findings from infant research. This necessity for representation also underpins why Bion's pre-concepts need to be realized, as he puts it, to become psychically active. They require representation to function.

    The capacity to form representations, which centrally map an afferent stimulus, acts as an immaterial barrier to brain activity. This is analogous, in a way, to the blood-brain barrier, in that beyond a certain morphogenetic level of brain structures, based on the systemic properties of the human organ brain, representation formation commences in the cerebral cortex. This marks a categorical leap, giving rise to a self-contained system: the world of representations. This domain within the total structure of the brain is where self-reflective consciousness arises, on the basis of representational, phantasmatically organized structure formation, as I have described. Mental content is thus confined to what has formed into a representation.

This aspect touches upon the relationship between the motivational, mental drive structure of the psyche – whose task is the protection of the ego – and its somatic substrate, namely, the comprehensive complex of bodily, humoral, neurobiological, and instinct-driven conditions within which the psyche operates. In my view, this relationship can be distinctly defined; it involves the inner external world impacting the ego in its fundamental role as the organ and subject of perception. The ego processes this stimulation by forming representations within its own set of lawful principles, which I have detailed. A prime example of this would be sexuality, where the somatic sexual instinct is psychically organized within the phantasmatization of the life and death drives, and thus within the context of oedipal content and structure. Therefore, the stimulation by the inner external world, in its general significance, is not different from that by the outer external world of the out-of-body reality.

What distinctively differentiates the representations of the inner external world, or body representations, is the process of primary identification. I interpret this process as the projection of the sensation of aliveness, inherently linked to body representations, onto the primary object initially perceived as inanimate, followed by the introjection of the now

81

animate object representation. Through this mechanism, the perception of the primary object as animate emerges alongside a nascent self-awareness of the ego as animate.[2] It is likely that primary identification is intimately related to the process of primal attachment to the partial object of the breast.

The critical phenomenon is that the brain establishes a foundational structure bound to representations, serving as the structural framework within which mental operations occur and consciousness emerges. Mental functioning is not possible outside this framework; it acts as the coordinate system. The key for comprehending this fundamental structure is the oedipal theme, encompassing its early and preliminary forms, as delineated in this work.

The themes and structural positions outlined in the foregoing can be seen as the living phantasmatic coordinate system of the realm of human consciousness, encompassing both functionally conscious and functionally unconscious content. This coordinate system acts as the background matrix for the subjective, personal constructions from which the individual ego builds his life and inner world. What the analyst must uncover, elucidate, and interpretatively transform in the patient's material and transference is essentially this matrix.

2. The entire energetic, functional, and structural differentiation of the psyche stems from the foundational conflict of the ego, which emerges from perception, with its self-suspension in the intended fusion with the object. The primary hypothesis from which I started out, posits that psychic life initiates

---

2 I thank Dr. Andreas Sadjiroen for pointing out that here a definition for primary identification is necessary to describe how the character of the animateness of the representations of the inner external world comes about.

with the central nervous system's ability to form neuronal representations perceived by the subject, this perception constituting the ego function. To the extent that the discipline-specific logical application of this primary hypothesis succeeds in describing the full range of the psychical, and thus can be considered deductively proven through this capacity, it logically follows in retrospect that the inception of psychic life – which, after all, we cannot directly evidence – should indeed be presumed to align with the basic theorem, that is, to stem from perception. This is particularly relevant to the discussion on an initial pre-schizoid phase of psychic development.

3. A significant implication of these considerations is that since all mental functional forms and pathologies can be elucidated through the genetic sequence of this system's self-organization and its lawful deviations, it logically follows that the cerebral cortex, responsible for forming representations and serving as the foundation of this system, should be considered a tabula rasa. It operates solely under the laws emerging from the perceptual system itself, without influence from any other intrinsic factors to determine the basic structure formation of the psyche, culminating in the Oedipus complex. The examination of this structure formation, its governing laws, and their therapeutic modification constitutes the realm of psychoanalysis.

    This perspective, viewing the cortex as a blank slate, a tabula rasa, is similarly reached by Panksepp and Solms from a strictly neurobiological standpoint (see Solms 2021a, p. 560ff).

4. Given that this entire process adheres to logical and causal necessity, it embodies the characteristics of a Natural Law, specifically governing the formation and functional structuring

of the psyche, or more precisely, of the mental realm. This statement extends beyond the traditional boundaries associated with the concept of Natural Law, particularly in terms of material quantifiability. Within the conventional framework, the realm of the mental would ostensibly lack Natural Laws, given the complexities surrounding the issue of material quantifiability. However, such a stance is insufficient, as it would unjustly exclude the entire natural domain of the psyche – a domain central to the human species – from being governed by Natural Laws.

I draw upon the expanded understanding of modern physics, which shifts the foundational reference from matter to information. In the subatomic realms of physics, one encounters particles devoid of detectable mass, defined solely through their statistical presence within certain functional contexts, time units, and areas – essentially, through their informational properties. With this perspective, the criterion of material quantifiability, once central to legitimacy, is set aside in favor of information that delineates functional contexts. Given that psychoanalysis also explores a domain of nature that is invisible, defining our regularities in purely functional terms, there is no reason to exclude our field from this broader interpretation of Natural Laws.[3]

It is a bold step, but one that psychoanalysis should embrace, to assert that we have, in fact, articulated the Natural Laws of the psyche.

---

3 I would like to thank Dr. Franz Zimmermann for clarifying the rigorous philosophical constraints of the classical definition of Natural Law.

84

Essay 2

On the Metapsychology of the
Earliest Mental State

Frances Tustin, in 1972 and 1981, described primary psychogenic encapsulated autism, necessitating an expansion of psychoanalytic theory regarding psychic structure formation, as this form of autism cannot be adequately explained by the splitting concept of the object relation. Melanie Klein posited that the good-bad split of the infantile paranoid-schizoid position represents the fundamental functional form of the psyche. She argued that this split arises directly from the dichotomy between experiences of pleasure and unpleasure, or love and hate, corresponding to the death drive and the life drive, respectively. Klein regarded the infantile paranoid-schizoid position in this sense as the rock bottom of psychic structure formation.

As outlined, my primary hypothesis proposes that from the moment the ontogenetic maturation of the central nervous system enables the first sensory perceptions, these perceptions are inherently bipolar in structure. They comprise two poles: the perceiving subject and the perceived itself, or in other words, the representation. Here, perception is fundamentally understood as the capacity to form a central representation of an afferent stimulus. I introduce the operational hypothesis that, in psychoanalytic terms, the perceiving subject equates directly to the archaic, primordial ego, while the perceived – namely, the representation – corresponds to the archaic, primordial object. *This marks the commencement of the dimension of the psychical.*

By "operational hypothesis," I refer to the notion that this assumption can only be retrospectively justified based on the clinical plausibility of the outcomes that stem from this hypothesis. This implies that the hypothesis's validity is assessed not through direct evidence or a priori reasoning, but through the coherence, relevance, and applicability of the insights and explanations it provides in a clinical context.

In the first section of this work, I have illustrated how the primary hypothesis regarding the emergence of ego and object from the act of perception logically necessitates a comprehensive theory of psychic structure formation and a theory concerning the genesis of psychic drives. The fundamental premise is that from the primary positing of ego and object, with the addition of need pressure – that is, of unpleasure – on the part of the ego, there inevitably arises the wish for fusion with the object. This is because the object, being the only thing given apart from the ego, must be regarded as the place which contains the means for the annulment of need. Within this context, fusion is understood as the most archaic, primitive, and thus foundational form of appropriation.

I have detailed that this sought-after fusion would result in the annulment of the dimension of the psychical that had just originated from perception, given that perception – and thereby the realm of the psychical – is inherently bound to the distinction and thus separateness of ego and object. Consequently, I have equated this fusional impulse with the psychic death drive and demonstrated that all subsequent structural development is dedicated solely to achieving one primary objective: to safeguard the separation between the ego and the object. Furthermore, I have outlined how psychopathology can systematically be understood through the various strategies an ego, under the influence of the death drive, might employ to compromise and undermine this separation from the object.

The compliance of a proposition with a comprehensive and consistent, i.e., contradiction-free, theory that is logically rigorously derived from a simplest primary hypothesis and validated at key points by clinical practice, represents an alternative to the empirical verification of truth content through randomized controlled trials, within the context of the theory of science. This method of proof should be pursued by psychoanalysis, although until now, it was believed challenging – or, rather, impossible – to identify such a basic primary hypothesis, self-explanatory in nature, that could serve as a foundation for the entire psychoanalytic theoretical edifice and its supporting empirical evidence. The discoveries made by Tustin have altered this perspective. *The act of perception* offers such a foundational basis. The clinic of primary psychogenic encapsulated autism and the theoretical deductions derived from this clinic are the critical elements that have facilitated and indeed necessitated the development of a metapsychology revised in this manner. Thus, primary psychogenic encapsulation autism is identified as the missing link for this new metapsychology.

Tustin demonstrated that primary psychogenic encapsulation autism stems from a scenario in which the ego undergoes the traumatic experience of the object withdrawing from fusion – essentially, a premature and thus traumatic realization of separateness from the object. Tustin referred to this withdrawing object as the "not-me" object. In response to its perceived rejection, the ego in primary autism forecloses this not-me object. As a result, the connection to the object as such is severed, leading to a stagnation of psychic development, given that this development relies on the conflictual interaction with the object. It's crucial to recognize that in cases of primary encapsulation autism, these processes occur in the very earliest days of psychic life – beginning intrauterinely, in any event, before primal attachment is established. Tustin describes these children as hypersensitive, hyperpermeable, and thus hypervulnerable, making them particularly prone to experiencing a traumatic rejection by the object, regardless of the presence of additional accidental factors.

Tustin's clinical depiction of primary psychogenic encapsulated autism reveals that this condition is founded on a unified, rather than a split, object representation. This framework alone elucidates how the foreclosure of what Tustin terms the "not-me" object results in a total arrest of psychic development. Once the representation is split within the good-bad dichotomy, foreclosure can no longer precipitate such a complete breakdown, as one aspect of the object invariably remains external to the foreclosure.

In the first part of this paper, I demonstrated that object splitting is intricately linked to the development of object constancy. Object constancy refers to the neurologically determined capacity to compare successive representations of the primary object over time. It serves as the foundational requirement for retaining the counterpart to the split representation within the mental backdrop, enabling the concept of object splitting. Given that I characterize the pre-schizoid phase as psychic functioning under conditions where object constancy has not yet been established, the foreclosure of the object is inherently tied to the pre-schizoid phase – or to a level of psychic functioning that aligns with the pre-schizoid phase.

Similarly, the longing for fusional unity with the primary object, the rejection of which Tustin identifies as the catalyst for foreclosure, is only conceivable in relation to a uniform, that is, an unsplit and – more crucially – uniquely given object. Only under these conditions does the pursuit of fusional unity as an aspired total solution become logical. Hence, the desire for fusion also genetically stems from the pre-schizoid phase, which, in terms of the object, is defined by these two specific criteria: uniformity, meaning the object is not split, and the fact that the current representation of the object is the only given thing due to the absence of comparative capability – namely, the yet-to-be-established object constancy.

In light of these reflections, it appears crucial to acknowledge that fusion and foreclosure, at the unconscious level, are intrinsically tied to the pre-schizoid level of functioning. Therefore, when fusion and foreclosure are psychically activated, it indicates that the pre-schizoid level of functioning is unconsciously constelated and operative. This illustrates the principle that all ontogenetic layers of the psyche at any one time do always participate in life and can come to the fore, even if the conditions under which they were initially formed have long become structurally outdated. Consequently, a psychic state can temporarily predominate where the object cannot yet be split, and this object faces the ego as the only thing that exists and as the source of all possible satisfaction. This scenario sets the stage for the desire for fusion and thereby for the death drive, which, as I have elucidated, coincides with narcissism insofar as in fusion, ego and object become identical. In essence, when the death drive is active, the pre-schizoid phase is inevitably also active, because the death drive, as demonstrated in the first part of this work, embodies the ego of the pre-schizoid phase.

Tustin has characterized primary psychogenic autism as a "two stage illness": "I have come to see that autism is a protective reaction that develops to deal with the stress associated with a traumatic disruption of an abnormal perpetuated state of adhesive unity with the other. (...) First, there is a perpetuation of dual unity, and then the traumatic disruption of this and the stress that it arouses" (1994b, p14). Elsewhere in the same work she has also referred to this "dual unity" as "adhesive-at-oneness" or "adhesive equation" (1994b, p15). And, "Flowing-over-at-oneness is the process by which the illusion of primal unity is maintained" (1981, p80). From these observations, it's evident that Tustin's theory indeed revolves around a fusional movement and phantasy. Hence, I refer to the fusion of the ego with the representation of the primary object as the objective of the first stage of autistic disorder.

When attempting to interpret Tustin's insights within a metapsychological framework, it becomes essential to acknowledge a primary condition characterized by three key aspects: first, the object cannot yet be split; second, the primary object is perceived as the only given in a total and global sense; and third, the driving pathogenic factor in relation to this primary object is the desire for fusion. If we are forced by the clinic of psychogenic encapsulated primary autism to assume a mental condition prior to the good-bad split of the object – the pre-schizoid phase –, we are thus at the beginnings of a new metapsychology.

From these reflections, a crucial distinction emerges in relation to Tustin's characterization of primary autism as a "two-stage illness," particularly when she discusses an "abnormal perpetuated state of adhesive unity with the other" (op.cit.). This phrase implies the actual existence of such a state of adhesive unity, suggesting that it can be abnormally prolonged or continued, i.e. perpetuated. However, it's vital to recognize that it is actually about the *phantasy* of fusional unity, rather than a concrete, factual state. In essence, it represents an intense longing. A real fulfillment of this longing would precipitate the collapse of the dimension of the psychical and the disintegration of the ego. This looming threat, rather than the realization of fusion, prompts the emergence of the not-me object, manifesting the primary object in a guise that explicitly rejects and avoids fusion. This, in turn, traumatically underscores the separateness of ego and object, what Tustin refers to as "the traumatic disruption of dual unity" (op.cit.).

In my analysis and terminology, this traumatic disruption, triggered by the not-me object, results from the life drive's activity. This drive acts as a safeguard for the self-preservation of the dimension of the psychical, striving to avert fusion. From the object's standpoint, this protective activity of the life-drive manifests in the context of autistic pathology as the not-me object; from the ego's perspective, it appears as the terror of ego dissolution accompanying the urge of fusion.

The objective of this current study is to demonstrate how the structural conditions inherent in the pre-schizoid phase precisely align with the symptomatic manifestations of primary autism, or how, in another part, these manifestations directly arise from these structural conditions. This investigation seeks to bridge the understanding between the foundational psychic structures of the pre-schizoid phase and the observable clinical symptoms of primary autism, elucidating how the latter is a direct consequence of the former.

In this context, it's important to revisit and clarify the characteristics of the primary object of perception, a topic I previously addressed in the first part of this work. The initial, sensory-based object that emerges directly with the activation of the cerebral perceptual function initially bears no relation to a human – or even animate – counterpart. This primary object is rooted purely in sensory perception, devoid of any anthropomorphic or animate attributes, reflecting the most basic and uninterpreted level of sensory input as processed by the nascent perceptual capacities of the brain. It is the precipitation of unassigned coenesthetic stimuli, originating from the external world as well as being of proprioceptive, enteroceptive or central nervous provenance, held together solely by their temporal contiguity. No distinction can yet be made between an inside and an outside of the body or person, and a concept of reality does not yet exist. It is about the level of the very first object representations in the sense of the precipitation of the sensory stimulations organized – that is consolidated – only by simultaneity within a primordial constitution, which does not yet know any differentiated mental contents, i.e. phantasies, thoughts or symbols, apart from the sensory stimulation, because the mental space necessary for this has not yet been built up. Notably, the animation of the object in the process of primary identification has not yet taken place.

One might raise the question of why these primary afferents should be considered inanimate, especially if they originate, at least in part, from certain areas or functions of the living body. Wouldn't their origin imbue them with the quality of animation? However, I maintain that the characteristic of being animated becomes perceptible only at the level of partial object organization, which coincides with a corresponding integration of body representations. Prior to this, it is individual afferent signals of various proprioceptive and exteroceptive origins that, due to their coincidental temporal contiguity, amalgamate into a primary object representation. This primary object, by its nature, is inanimate or, at the very least, not explicitly animate.

The process of vivification emerges specifically from primary identification. This process involves projecting the sensation of aliveness, associated with the evolving integration of body representations, onto the primary object, which is initially perceived as inanimate. Following this projection, there is a re-introjection of the now animate object representation back into the self. Through this mechanism, the individual begins to perceive the primary object as animate. Moreover, through the identification that accompanies this re-introjection, a foundational self-experience of the ego as an animate entity is formed. As previously mentioned, it is likely that primary identification is deeply interconnected with the process of primal attachment to the partial object of the breast.

Next, conclusions about the fundamental nature of the primary relations between ego and object arise from my considerations: Inasmuch as stimulations from all possible sensory sources converge upon this primary object, and these stimulations are interconnected solely by their temporal contiguity, this primary object incorporates stimuli originating both from the subject's sphere and the general environment, *particularly from the surrounding maternal organism.* Notably, according to established findings, we find ourselves still within the intrauterine situation regarding the origins of perceptual function and, according to my hypothesis, the genesis of psychic experience. From this standpoint, these amalgamated object constructions, encountered, for instance, in the treatment of autistic children or severe regressions, convey the semblance of a symbiotic form of experience.

It is crucial to underscore that, from a metapsychological standpoint, this perspective is misleading. The primary object is the primary object – in terms of what is perceived – irrespective of the origin of its sensory elements. The primary experience is not symbiotic in the sense of a fundamental indistinctness between ego and object representation. This misconception gives rise to a theoretically consequential error, as misinterpreted clinical data have led to the presumption of a primordial symbiotic chaos where somatic stimuli, self and object representations are in an undistinguished confusion. Descriptively accurate, yes, but this is precisely the primary object.

The theoretical framework adopted has a profound influence on the approach to clinical situations, as the analytic attitude can significantly differ based on the underlying assumptions about the psyche's primary structural constitution. Assuming a factual symbiotic fusion as this foundation diverges markedly from understanding that a symbiotic representation possesses object character. If one assumes the former, the analytical work might erroneously focus on disentangling this presumed innate symbiotic fusion between the self and the other, while the objectal interpretation acknowledges that the seeming fusional chaos is a very normal step within development, i.e. without psychopathological significance.

On its corresponding level of the structurally simplest organization of mental constitution, the primary object is the only thing that exists. An outside beyond the primary object is not yet conceivable, as such an outside presupposes the experience of time as the correlate of an incipient object constancy. Time enables comparison and therefore allows the notion of the outside to emerge. The primary object, in the primordial condition before the representational object constancy is achieved, is for the primary ego *the universe, the All-there-is, outside of which nothing exists*, since no comparison with previous or subsequent representations is possible. Its characteristics are totality and globality.

Object constancy serves as the foundation for both memory and the perception of time. Likewise, it underlies the ability to perceive space, encompassing the recognition of distance and three-dimensionality. The emergence of spatial perception results from the *sequence* of the momentary representations of the primary object in object constancy. Thus, in the phase preceding the acquisition of object constancy, perception is two-dimensional, akin to the distanceless adhesive contact with surfaces experienced by primary psychogenic autists, whose disease-causing traumatization occurred in precisely this first phase of psychic development and whose functional mode remained fixated on this level.

The cognitive categories of space and time, therefore, emanate from object constancy. In other words, within the framework of this first level of psychic functioning before object constancy, we are in an experience outside of space and time. It is mainly this characteristic – in addition to the very archaic, two-dimensional modalities of perception tied to immediate sensory experience – that makes the forms of primary autism located in this stage so difficult to understand and to access. To complete the picture, it is essential to add that without the dimensions of space and time, the ability to relate to other bodies is not possible. The absence of space and time means that the object as an other body cannot be conceptualized, rendering primal attachment unattainable. This is the situation of the psychogenic primary encapsulated autists.

By extension, these lines of reasoning should be applied to the ego itself. The ego, as the subject of perception, appears, from a perspective related to subjective experience, just at the most elementary level of its function in every individual moment in time, in its full potential identity and energetic wholeness. Even though it might appear deficient and fragmented when observed externally, the primary ego lacks reflective distance from itself. There is no relativization of the ego through the comparison of its states in time, just as there is no concept of an external dimension to the object and thus no relativization of the object. In essence, the criteria of totality and globality not only apply to the primary object but equally to the primary ego.

Significantly, this consideration has direct implications for the viewpoint that regards the infantile notion of omnipotence as a defensive formation against the experience of primary helplessness. Viewing this as an adultomorphism, the early infantile experience lacks the ability to recognize its objective helplessness, requiring access to reality, which is not present in this primordial state. The situation is quite the opposite: infantile omnipotence is primary, bestowed with tremendous force, and stems from the absence of being bound to any kind of condition. This instance highlights how theoretical understanding may significantly influence clinical practice: Assuming primary helplessness as a directly felt experience can result in what might be termed a sentimental misunderstanding of the early childhood situation. Such an approach risks neglecting the critical aspect of omnipotence.

The theme on both the ego and the object side is paradoxically absoluteness, as no insight into the conditionality of reality is yet possible. This paradox arises because, despite the child being objectively in a state of maximum dependence and helplessness at this early stage – seemingly contradictory to the experience of absoluteness, omnipotence, and unlimited abundance – the lack of insight into conditionality fosters an experience of absoluteness as the primary psychological condition. It is this contradiction that has made it so difficult to conceptualize this earliest constitution. While the body may be shaken by organismic despair, a traumatic experience of lack, on the psychic level, this lack, in the context of an experience of the primary object as the embodiment of absolute good, generates an acute phantasy of fusion. This, in turn, gives rise to the panic of ego-loss. Thus, this panic is not a direct response to the organismic deficiency; rather, the notion of a direct response to organismic deficiency ignores a crucial phantasmatic intermediate step – the fusional phantasy. This missing element introduces the entire issue of psychic processing.

Just like the concepts of a symbiotic primary relationship and primary helplessness, the theorem of primary narcissism presents another critical point for understanding the problematic impact of theoretical frameworks on basic clinical approaches and therapeutic strategies. Freud's pseudopodia model, comprising the idea of a primary narcissistic concentration of the entire libido within the ego, emerged as theoretical response to clinical encounters with archaic feelings of omnipotence and narcissistic withdrawal. Without the foundational hypothesis that the psyche originates from perception, and without the ensuing conclusion that ego *and* object arise simultaneously and equitably, alongside the implication of an energetic parity between ego and object, the notion of a primary concentration of libido in the ego naturally presents itself as the metapsychological underpinning for the concept of omnipotence. Furthermore, without the additional theoretical deduction of a pre-schizoid phase characterized by a neurologically determined inability to compare across time and space, it becomes challenging to comprehend why both the primary ego and the primary object, in this initial form of psychic functioning, exist without mutual competition, both embodying absolute significance – manifested through the theme of omnipotence from the ego's perspective, and the qualities of totality and globality from the object's standpoint.

These considerations are far from being merely academic. It is through this metapsychological framework that we can clinically understand why, in the case of primary autism of the encapsulation type, an ego imbued with phantasies of omnipotence feels compelled to foreclose the object representation in response to its withdrawal. It is precisely this act of desperate foreclosure of the only given object that signifies the object as being laden with a maximum of expectation, a scenario that is only comprehensible in the context of a primary object characterized by totality and globality. The entire clinical picture of primary autism underscores the involvement of an archaic ego within a fundamental conflict with an archaic form of object representation, indicating from the outset a dynamic involving a high-energy ego and a high-energy object representation. Theoretically, nothing better illustrates this scenario than the concept of a confrontation between ego and object that arises directly from perception.

In this pre-schizoid phase, therefore, we observe three key characteristics: first, the ego *and* the object hold absolute significance; second, the phase is defined by the constitutive criterion of being timeless and spaceless; and third, the primary object cannot be split according to the good-bad dichotomy because a splitting alternative to this primary object is inconceivable due to the undeveloped object constancy – that is, the absence of a concept of time and space.

If these propositions about the primary level of functioning of the mental apparatus are accurate, it follows that within this primary constitution, there can be no representation of an experience of unpleasure, or unlust, as a bad, rejecting object. According to our primary hypothesis, the initial situation is such that the primary ego, in addressing an experience of lack or deficiency, can only identify the remedy for this deficiency in the primary object, since the primary object is the only entity given outside of itself – that is, outside of the ego. Consequently, the ego attempts to assimilate or incorporate this means of remedying the deficiency through fusion with the primary object.

If the primary object of the preschizoid phase serves as the means to remedy all deficiencies, then *this primary object of the pre-schizoid phase must represent completeness and abundance. There is no conception of the primary object as a representation of lack.* Hence, the primary object, prior to the development of object constancy, is the preambivalent object. There is no representation apart from this. The negative cannot yet be represented *in terms of an object representation* and only exists within psychic space as the pressure of anxiety that demands a change in the existing overall situation. In a phase before the potential for object splitting, a direct objectal representation of a negative state would imply that the ego, in totality, is faced with a bad or evil cosmos. This is not compatible with the maintenance of life. The representation that most closely approximates a negative state, before the achievement of object constancy, is the autistic not-me object, that is, the representation of an object of abundance and completeness that withdraws from the ego.

Primary identification, as previously outlined, should be understood within the context of primal attachment, that is, the association of the primary object as the representation of absolute abundance and completeness with the experience or the pre-concept of the breast. This association leads to the emergence of the imago of the good breast and marks the commencement of psychosexual development.

To underscore this proposition for its significance, I assert that the imago of the good breast as the representation of the life-sustaining force and capacity emerges from the primal attachment of the pre-schizoid primary object, characterized by abundance and completeness, to the now evolving partial object of the breast and the preconceptual ideas associated with it. This association with the purely internal, autochthonous, or aboriginal representation of the pre-schizoid object of abundance and completeness endows – virtually inspires – the partial object of the breast with its paradigmatical quality of being the good object.

That the breast, through its biological function, produces the life-sustaining milk factually supports this association. However, for understanding the basic psychic functioning, it is crucial to recognize that biology alone is insufficient. To introduce the specifically psychical dimension, an additional process of imagination is required that goes beyond the purely instinctual level of biology. The realm of the imaginative, as I outlined in my work, builds itself up autonomously, starting from perception and grounded in the systemic properties of the human cerebral cortex. In primal attachment, the autochthonous and internally originated primary object connects for the first time with the external, real, and bodily object. As mentioned, this initiates psychosexual development. In encapsulated autism, this step cannot be taken.

Omnipotence of the ego and absolute completeness and abundance of the object, then, are the two defining criteria of the pre-schizoid phase, characterized by totality and globality. Tustin explicitly mentions that the motive behind the fusional efforts of autistic children is to maintain or restore omnipotent control over the object. The bodily sensations mediated by the autistic object, as well as by autostimulation, provide the child with the feeling that "(…) he had a perfect mother always with him who gave him ecstatic and instant sensual satisfaction" (1981, p 103).

The absolute dominion of omnipotence in the pre-schizoid phase further implies that frustration tolerance cannot develop under these conditions, as omnipotence negates the acceptance of frustration. This is reflected in the pathognomonic tendency of encapsulated autistic children to exhibit raging fits of temper tantrums and panicky anxiety. In the words of Tustin: "The constant use of Autistic Objects means that the psychotic child has little possibility of learning to tolerate frustration and to develop a more realistic evaluation of inner and outer stimuli which are felt to be life-threatening. When frustration impinges, tantrums pound through muscle and vein and cause the child to fear total annihilation. To counteract this deadly terror, he clutches a hard Autistic Object. He never learns to deal with bodily and mental irritation in a considered, thinking way" (1981, p110).

When Tustin discusses the pathological and rampant omnipotence of autistic children and their unawareness of their actual weakness and dependency, I interpret these not – as Tustin does – as pathological deviations from an original state of any kind. Instead, from my point of view, Tustin is here spelling out the globality and totality of experience in the pre-schizoid phase, where, as previously stated, the primary object constitutes the All, the universe, beyond which nothing else exists. Similarly, the ego perceives itself as unbounded and unconditioned, starkly contrary to its real neotenous helplessness and weakness, because it does not yet recognize its real limitations and is not yet identified with them. This forms the foundation of the experience of omnipotence. *Omnipotence, therefore, is not exclusive or specific to primary autism but is characteristic of the pre-schizoid phase, to which the autist remains fixated.*

By foreclosing the object, encapsulated autism halts further development and, through the use of the autistic object, disavows the perception of the defect created by the foreclosure, thereby denying the autistic hole. In this way, encapsulation autism preserves the pre-schizoid constitution and illustrates the tremendous psychic force generated when neither the object nor the ego is constrained or limited by reality. It is from this totality and globality that the powerful formative influence of this primordial condition of the pre-schizoid phase on subsequent psychic life originates.

When we discuss omnipotence as the defining quality of the ego in the pre-schizoid phase, the corresponding criterion for the object is its attribution of absolute fullness, completeness, and abundance. It is evident that this attribute of absolute completeness is the reason why, on one hand, the primary autistic ego seeks to achieve fusional unity with this object of completeness and, on the other hand, why the refusal of this fusion – namely, the object's transformation into the withdrawing not-me object – leads so inexorably to its unconditional foreclosure. *Here, too, we encounter the scenario where the primary autist adopts the central characteristic of the object from the pre-schizoid phase as a representation of completeness and, upon the emergence of the not-me object, responds by foreclosure, in line with his pathological intent of disavowal of separateness from the object.* The totality of this foreclosure corresponds to the totality and globality of the primary object of the pre-schizoid phase and the association of this totality and globality with the attribute of absolute, thus total and global, completeness.

We are, after all, exploring the connection between the deductions made from the hypothesis that the psychical originates from perception and the phenomenology of primary autistic disorder. A crucial perspective in this discussion is that, for theoretical reasons, there must exist an absolute dependency on immediate sensory experience, and thus on two-dimensionality and tactility, in the pre-schizoid phase. This stems from the fact that this earliest experience directly arises from the perceptual function. The capability to distance oneself from immediate sensory experience by the breakthrough to the perception of distance and the perception of space, only emerges through the ability to compare successive object representations in time and space, i.e., through object constancy.

Encapsulated autism corroborates this understanding. By foreclosing the representation of the primary object, the psychogenetically encapsulated autist is unable to take the developmental step towards comparing object representations in time and space. Consequently, as clinical evidence shows, he remains trapped in being tied to the sensorial. This explicit attachment to immediate, distanceless sensoriality – namely, to tactility – reflects the autistic disavowal of separateness from the object.

This attachment to the immediate, two-dimensional, and thus predominantly tactile sensory experience, outside of time and space, contributes significantly to the distinct phenomenology of primary autistic symptomatology. Besides those symptoms that specifically pertain to the disavowal of separateness from the object – such as the autistic sensation object, the autistic sensation shapes, and imitative behavior – it conditions the challenging accessibility of these children, as described by authors such as Frances Tustin, Didier Houzel, Maria Rhode, Joshua Durban, Suzanne Maiello, Anne Alvarez, Marie-Christine Laznik and others.

To elaborate on the theme of tactile attachment in primary autism and its connection to the autistic disavowal of separation from the object, I will include some quotations from the literature. Tustin (1990, p 218) writes: „In autistic states, the sense of touch over-rides sight and hearing." And Maiello: "The crucial point is that tactile sensations are misused to shut out any other kind of sensuous experience, because *touch is the only sense that ensures the absence of distance from the object*" (1997, p 10; emph. SM). "Distance is the very thing autistic children cannot bear. It was the primitive experience of separateness that necessitated their radical self-protection against any awareness of space, and hence of 'not-me' experiences.

Although autistic children are neither blind nor deaf, they do not look or listen. They eliminate the normal functioning of the senses that are connected with distance by equating every potentially symbol-promoting experience with an a-symbolic 'no-space' tactile situation. As Tustin writes: 'I have come to realize that vision and hearing, as a result of the undue dominance of the sense of touch, become excessively imbued with tactile sensation' (1986, p 145)" (Maiello 1997, p 15).

In my view, it is erroneous to believe that the adherence to the sensory system, and thus to two-dimensionality and especially tactility, stems directly from autistic pathology itself – that is, *being a product* of the autistic pathological phantasmatization which disavows separateness from the object and consequently clings to tactility. It is more accurately a characteristic of the pre-schizoid phase, wherein the genesis of primary autistic pathology is situated, and arises, as mentioned, from the yet undeveloped capability to compare different states of the primary object, i.e., from the absence of object constancy. *The pathognomonic feature of primary autism, namely, the battle against separateness from the object, coincides with, adopts, and utilizes this two-dimensional sensoriality of the pre-schizoid phase and its associated elements – omnipotence, totality and globality, timelessness, and spacelessness.*

Through primary autism, which preserves this archaic pre-schizoid functional form of the psyche, we gain direct observational access to it, somewhat akin to being transported back to the era of the dinosaurs. Therefore, the absence of distance perception is not an invention by the autist in reaction to the not-me object – i.e. in reaction to the experience of separation from the object –, but rather the prevailing, ambient characteristic of the pre-schizoid phase. This characteristic is retained as a result of the foreclosure, the exclusion of the not-me object, that is, as the manifestation of denying separation from the object. However, the preservation of two-dimensionality is not a deliberate choice or decision but the outcome of the total decline of object representation following the foreclosure of the not-me object. This foreclosure leads to the decline of object representation as a whole, due to the totality and globality of the pre-schizoid phase. Here, the all-or-nothing principle applies. Consequently, object constancy cannot be achieved, and without object constancy, there is no concept of time, space, three-dimensionality, perception of the other body, and, therefore, no primal attachment. The child remains stuck in the pre-schizoid phase.

Due to the absence of distance perception, it is necessary to assume that in this pre-schizoid mental environment hearing, seeing and smelling – i.e. the distance modalities – within the framework of two-dimensionality are co-enaesthetically translated into tactile sensations. Clinical observations support this perspective: the distance perception modalities are effectively nullified by the primary autist in their intrinsic character and shifted into the tactile domain: *The elimination of distance modalities, also in this context, is not an invention of the autist but rather an intrinsic characteristic of the pre-schizoid phase. The primary experience of the autist is bound and tied to this phase and, secondarily, he exploits and clings to it as a strategy for disavowing separateness from the object.*

In this way, the autist turns, here too, against the recognition of the separation of the source of stimulation from his own body or from the immediate ego, challenging the perceptual basis of acknowledging separateness from the object. This disavowal of perceiving distance directly impacts the experience of dimensionality: the third dimension, space – and crucially, interior space – may not be experienced since space is equated with distance and, therefore, separation. Thus, the notions of inside and outside are inaccessible, just as the criteria of animate and inanimate would imply the recognition of an existence separate from the ego and are therefore, by the encapsulated autist, excluded.

Tustin and others (Haag 1985, Haag et al. 2005, Winnicott 1949, Bick 1968, 1986) described the severe existential fears that autistic children face: dissolving, liquefying, leaking, falling to pieces, falling forever, having no skin or a skin full of holes, having the skin torn away, burning, freezing, suffocating, losing the sense of time and space, of orientation, losing a part or parts of the body. J.Durban (2014) speaks here of "anxieties of being". Durban (2021) has further described the, as he calls them, osmotic-diffuse anxieties, an even more archaic type of anxiety in which the toxic attack on the ego is experienced as coming from everywhere and nowhere.

As long as the ego engages with the object from a position of assured separateness, it is safeguarded precisely by the objectality of the object. This is because the only internal threat to the ego arises from the elimination of its separateness from the object, which would result in the dissolution of the representations of ego and object due to the breakdown of the perceptual function. Thus, the primary goal of psychic structural development is to establish a structurally guaranteed non-identity of ego and object.

I thus believe that the anxieties of being, and the osmotic-diffuse anxieties express the *loss of the object's protective function* in a fusional process. In my view, they represent the decomposition, the damage, the disintegration, the dismantling of the object representation in fusion – that is, not merely representing somehow rudimentary preforms of the object relation. This impairment of the object representation results both from the fusional process itself and from the subsequent autistic foreclosure of the object. This perspective is crucial in illuminating the nature of autistic symptomatology: primary autism is, above all, a syndrome of deficiency, not merely a syndrome of developmental arrest (though it is also that). The intact object serves as the protective mantle of the psyche and, in this sense, likely represents the primal form of containment, in the protection of which the destined ontogenetic transformations of the ego can occur.

This logically implies that the object presents itself in its complete metapsychological identity and energetic integrity and wholeness at the moment of the initial act of perception. As it follows from the nature of perception, this act is immediately and inherently manifested as separatedness of the perceived primary object from the perceiving ego, regardless of how archaic and undifferentiated its functional and structural form might be. Dynamically and structurally, it is, without reservation, the psychoanalytic object.

This leads me to another crucial point where the correspondence between the theory of the pre-schizoid phase and the clinical understanding of autistic disorders becomes evident: I have demonstrated that the first mental representation is formed at a specific neurological level of development of the cerebral cortex, based on sensory afferents of the most diverse origins – encompassing both internal bodily and external sources – which coincide at a particular moment in time. From this developmental history, it follows that these initial representations – the manifestations of the primary object – should be considered inanimate, just as the primary ego does not initially perceive itself as explicitly animate. The primary object and the primary ego are only imbued with life during the process of primary identification.

These insights into the process of primary identification and the associated vivification are mirrored in the clinical observations of autistic disorders. Here, the bodily experienced deficit resulting from the object's withdrawal – that is, from the emergence of the not-me object, followed by the foreclosure against the not-me object – is perceived by the encapsulated autist as an inanimate hole. This hole, due to its inanimate nature, does not change. Conversely, the confusional autist perceives this deficit as a wound, indicating that primary identification and thus the experience of vivification have already occurred in this case. Similarly, the encapsulated autist also experiences his own ego as inanimate. This presents a clear dichotomy between animate and inanimate within clinical manifestations, serving as the discriminatory criterion between these two very distinct clinical pictures: encapsulated and confusional autism.

This dichotomy also emerges completely in the same sense from the theoretical considerations regarding the pre-schizoid phase, highlighting the relevance of these theoretical insights to our clinical observations in treating children with psychogenic encapsulated autism and confusional autism. Specifically, these considerations suggest a clinically and theoretically significant implication: in primary encapsulated autists, primary identification – and hence the primal attachment to the breast – has not yet occurred, as evidenced by the inanimate concept of the autistic hole. This distinction is crucial for determining the onset of this disorder, a question that has been a recurrent focus of Frances Tustin's work.

As said, the clinical evidence for the existence of the pre-schizoid phase is to be seen in the primary psychogenic encapsulated autism described by Tustin as the first and most severe form of a mental illness. The key pathogenic moment in this context, as Tustin posits, is the ego's premature and traumatic encounter with a not-me object that equates to a premature and thus traumatic experience of separateness from the object – in my terminology, the encounter with a primary object that actively withdraws from the ego's fusional demands. From my perspective, this represents the defensive action of the life drive against the fusional impulses of the death drive. This traumatically disrupts the illusion of omnipotent control over the object, an illusion that is essential for healthy psychological development.

The fusional phantasy on which the illusion of omnipotent control over the object is based acts as a defense against the traumatic fear stemming from the experience of lack. This organismic, physiological fear is the primary driver of psychological development. When the fusional phantasy collapses – manifested as the encounter with the not-me object – the ego is left unprotected against the physiological experience of lack. Frances Tustin has specifically pointed out that children who are hypersensitive, hyperpermeable, and therefore hypervulnerable due to their constitutional disposition, are at a higher risk of encountering the not-me object and, consequently, of developing autism, as in these cases, in other words, the organismic anxiety becomes particularly intense.

The issue is most succinctly captured in Frances Tustin's remarks about her well-known young patient, John:

"But why have the object-seeking, shape-making propensities of the human mind been diverted into such unfortunate channels? (…) To understand this, we need to enquire into the origins of psychogenic autism. The first autistic child I had in intensive psychotherapy shed light on this for me.

When he was speaking, having been mute at the outset of treatment, this child John, as I have called him, alerted me to what he referred to as 'the black hole with the nasty prick'. It became clear that this had precipitated the autism (Tustin, 1972).

4-year-old John's revelations to me were stimulated by seeing a friend of his mother feeding her baby at the breast. The gist of what he conveyed to me was that, as an infant, he had taken for granted that the nipple experienced as an extension to his tongue (the 'button' as he called it), was part of his mouth. It had been an unbearable shock when he found that this was not so, and so was not always present and under his control. He showed me that this loss of the nipple-tongue and the burning rage it had aroused, had caused his mouth to become what he called 'a black hole with a nasty prick' " (1988 p 94f).

And elsewhere:

"there seems to [be] a hole in the breast where the 'button' had been. Since [John's] mouth had been undifferentiated from the breast, it leaves a 'hole' in his mouth also" (1986, p. 81).

The hole experienced by John was understood by Tustin, within a context based on particular vulnerability, as the manifestation of a premature and, therefore, traumatic experience of separation, which had initiated and caused the autistic foreclosure of the object. While this interpretation holds validity, my theoretical viewpoint, which emphasizes the significance of fusion and the defense against it as central to psychic conflictuality, suggests a deeper understanding. *The connection between mouth, tongue, nipple, and breast is seen as the bodily and sensory representation of the fusional experience, insofar as this mouth-tongue-nipple-breast connection represents the seamless continuity between the child's body and the mother's body.* The mouth-tongue-nipple-breast connection represents the core sensory embodiment of fusion at the pre-schizoid level, given its direct relation to the life-sustaining and security-providing act of breastfeeding. Here, the fusional phantasy of the ego, which seeks to incorporate and appropriate the object as the source and locus for the annulment of lack, finds its physical realization in the breastfeeding function.

In this paper, I posit that fusion – the merging of ego and object representations – represents the primary threat to the psyche. This is because fusion, culminating in the dissolution of the representations of ego and object, would precipitate the collapse of the perceptual function, which in turn is the basis of the dimension of the psychical. I view the entire psychic structure formation as a response to this threat. The life drive is the expression of both this peril and the defense against it. Consequently, I interpret the traumatic disruption of the mouth-tongue-nipple-breast connection as a psychic act deliberately aimed at countering the fusion embodied in this connection. This interpretation aligns with my description of the dynamics of the drives, specifically as a countermeasure to the fusionary objective of the death drive.

The cause for the traumatic disruption of the mouth-tongue-nipple-breast connection, the experience of the hole, and consequently, the autistic foreclosure of the object and the autistic withdrawal is found in this dynamic. The necessity of separation from the object must prevail; it forms the foundation of psychic development. John's inherent hypersensitivity, hyperpermeability, and thus hypervulnerability predisposed him to perceive this rupture as traumatic, leading him to react by retreating into autistic withdrawal.

Psychodynamically, the issue is not solely that children predisposed to primary autistic disorder experience separation too early and thus traumatically, nor is it solely about a specific vulnerability of these children, although both factors significantly contribute to the onset of the disorder. The critical dynamic element should be viewed intrapsychically and involves the overpowering intensity of the death drive, that is, the fusional impulse to merge with the primary object as the representation of all that is good, of absolute abundance, and as the representation of life preservation. This is what initiates the entire cascade of defensive reactions (such as the not-me object and its foreclosure) as well as the disintegration of the object representation, leading to autism. Constitutional vulnerability, as well as potentially experienced premature separation, cause the intensification of the

111

fusional tendency and, consequently, of the death drive. However, it is important to understand that both vulnerability and precocity are extrinsic factors that influence the intrinsic psychodynamics stemming from the problematic of the fusional desire.

With the emergence of separation, the 'black hole' is perceived as a representation of the traumatic nature of this separation, manifesting simultaneously in the mouth and within the breast itself. The latter is experienced as if there were an actual hole in the breast at the nipple's location, rendering it functionally destroyed. These reciprocal manifestations—namely, as a hole in the place of the mouth on one hand, and in the breast on the other—feature prominently in the treatment of autistic children. They are both the precipitate and outcome of the fusional experience, which, due to the fusional equation of ego and object, makes it unclear whether the problem originates from the subject or the object. Thus, the problem presents itself on both fronts.

The mouth-tongue-nipple-breast connection, as mentioned, represents the specific representational embodiment of fusion at the sensory and concrete level of the pre-schizoid phase. From this perspective, it holds significant importance and precision that John's phantasmatization in this context was the starting point for Frances Tustin's reflections on the psychodynamics of primary autism.

Revisiting the theme of this chapter, specifically addressing what aspects of autistic symptomatology are inherently linked to authentic autistic pathodynamics versus those reflecting the conditions of the pre-schizoid phase, the purely sensory depiction of the fusional phantasy via the mouth-tongue-nipple-breast connection exemplifies the pre-schizoid attachment to immediate sensorial experiences. In contrast, the trauma-induced autistic hole and the subsequent foreclosure of the object pertain more directly to the autistic experience in a narrower sense.

The anxieties of being and the osmotic-diffuse anxieties represent both the disintegration of the object representation in fusion and equally the inherent impossibility of fusion itself, highlighting the traumatic inevitability of separation from the object. Autistic objects and autistic sensual forms, along with autistic encapsulation – manifested as the autistic armor or carapace – are strategies to mitigate the traumatic impact of this separation, exemplified by John's 'black hole'. Similarly, Tustin's concept of adhesive equation and Meltzer's adhesive identification, as well as the notion of autistic bodily annexation (Rhode 2012), are employed to defend against both the act of separation and the existential anxieties (anxieties of being and osmotic-diffuse anxieties) tied to the traumatic experience of separation.

To summarize: If the autistic foreclosure of the object results in such a complete developmental arrest, it must reflect a psychic state in which the primary object is the only given in a total and global, thus unsplit, manner, as I have outlined in the characteristics of the pre-schizoid phase. Similarly, the notion of omnipotence emerges coherently both from my deduction of the implications of the primary hypothesis – that the origin of the psyche stems from perception – and from the phenomenology of encapsulated primary-autistic disorder. This also pertains to the absolute – and in this sense so-to-speak also omnipotent – significance of the primary object as the representation of abundance and completeness, which initially sparks the desire for fusion and subsequently leads to foreclosure. The same parallelism holds true for the connection of both the pre-schizoid phase and encapsulated autism to immediate two-dimensional sensory perception and tactility, and the consequent inaccessibility or, in the case of the autist, the explicit disavowal of distance perception.

Furthermore, the concept of the primary inanimate nature of the object is derived from the theory of the pre-schizoid phase and is corroborated by the clinical observations of psychogenic encapsulated autism. Additionally, the concept of the fundamentally protective function of the object, which is securely separated from the ego – a notion that emerges from my analysis of the psyche as derived from perception – is not only fully aligned with the clinical manifestations of primary autism, especially the anxieties of being and diffuse-osmotic anxieties, but the psychodynamics of the formation of the not-me object are rooted in this concept, as I have previously outlined. Last but not least, the pathognomonic mouth-tongue-nipple-breast connection, which represents the fusional phantasy at the pre-schizoid level and whose traumatic rupture stands paradigmatically at the heart of primary-autistic development, is also inconceivable without the pre-schizoid attachment to concretistic sensoriality.

Therefore, I regard primary psychogenic encapsulated autism as evidence for the existence of the pre-schizoid phase.

It is crucial to emphasize that within the psychodynamics of primary psychogenic encapsulated autism, there are no splitting mechanisms at play in the manner of the good-bad split characteristic of the paranoid-schizoid position. Instead, what we observe is a sequence and, eventually, a coexistence of mutually contradictory or, in a certain respect, mutually exclusive global states. These include, on one hand, the autistic foreclosure of the traumatic primary object – that is, the not-me object – which leaves a hole subsequently closed by the autistic object. On the other hand, there are imitative fusional practices and maneuvers aimed at denying the trauma associated with the emergence of the anti-fusional not-me object. Both mental states, as mentioned, are of an opposing nature but do not entail a splitting of either the ego or the primary object.

The coexistence of these mental states indicates a phase prior to achieving representational object constancy, a phase in which time and the comparison of different mental states over time, or temporal succession, are not yet perceived. In such a state, the currently active representation of the primary object in subjective experience becomes the All, beyond which nothing exists. Under these circumstances, the two opposing psychic states are unified by their shared traumatic context into a single experience wherein the primary object is foreclosed in its totality, and the ego, also in totality, enters pathognomonic imitative fusion with it. Consequently, the foreclosure of the traumatic not-me object – as manifested in the relationship with the compensatory autistic object – and imitative fusional relationship can coexist simultaneously. Due to their mutual assertion of absoluteness, these two fundamentally contradictory psychic movements – foreclosure and imitative fusion – can paradoxically coexist without disturbance. This is because the very experience of unconditional absoluteness creates a context in which contradiction and mutual exclusion find no representation. This results in the totality of the symptomatology encompassing the entire spectrum of experience, definitely blocking development. The condition of psychogenic early childhood autism of the encapsulation type is defined by this. It is not subject to a splitting mechanism.

This constellation demonstrates two key points:

1. The primary experience indeed occurs in a state of timelessness.
2. The primary object, in this initial phase of psychic life, truly possesses the character of totality and globality, as I have

described in the concept of a universe beyond which nothing exists.

This offers a metapsychologically rigorous explanation for the first form of mental illness. Conversely, I view this very sequence, along with the subsequent simultaneous occurrence of, on one hand, the foreclosure of the traumatic not-me version of the primary object and, on the other hand, reactive imitative fusion with its non-traumatic form of manifestation, as clinical evidence supporting the validity of my theories on the existence of a pre-schizoid phase. Such parallelism of contradictory object relations is only conceivable against the backdrop of a not yet established object constancy. This means that successive states of relation to the primary object cannot yet be compared and recognized as incompatible.

This constitutes a theoretical, metapsychological conclusion of primary significance. It validates the concept of an initial pre-schizoid phase in structural and psychosexual development. Theoretically, this insight represents the gain we achieve from our understanding of the earliest form of mental illness in psychogenic encapsulation autism. It confirms that our conclusions regarding psychic functioning at the primordial, most fundamental level are correct.

Through these considerations, we confront the implication of acknowledging a previously unrecognized earliest phase of psychic experiencing and functioning – the pre-schizoid phase – which is crucial for the psychoanalytic explanation of psychogenic primary encapsulation autism. This phase represents a level of unconscious structural phantasies that arise directly from the realities of perceptual functioning, thus bearing the characteristics of Natural Laws. They establish the psyche as a dimension and shape and determine further structural development. From a temporal perspective, the onset of this phase certainly coincides with the intrauterine form of existence, as perception neurologically begins within the womb.

Within our discussion centered on fundamental structural development, it's important to highlight that object constancy – the capability to compare object representations across time and space – marks *a first dramatic change in the mental level of functioning*. This transition, with the advent of object constancy, ends the compulsory bond to the unmediated sensorial experience, to two-dimensionality and tactility, and also to the unconditional, absolute experience of omnipotence. The phenomenology of primary encapsulation autism illustrates the dramatic nature of this shift, particularly because the incapsulated autist does not undergo this transformation.

With the establishment of object constancy, there is a pivotal transition from the pre-schizoid phase to the infantile paranoid-schizoid position. *The object can now be split according to the good-bad dichotomy*, allowing the negative to find its own representation, which stands in contrast to the representation of completeness and abundance. As mentioned, the ability to split the object relies on the capacity to maintain the counter-image to the activated split object within psychic space, a feat made possible only through object constancy. From this point forward, we enter the domain of established metapsychology. This represents a shift in functional level as significant as the change brought about by the depressive position later in development, which resolves the paranoid splitting of the object.

There are important interactions between theory and clinic: On one hand, informed by the theory of the pre-schizoid phase, it becomes clear – or rather is confirmed – that primary infantile autism is not, as in Mahler's conceptualization, a normal transitional phase through which all individuals necessarily pass. Primary autism has its pathognomonic unique feature in the foreclosure of the primary object. This is not normal development. On the other hand, the phenomenology of primary autistic disorders offers invaluable insights into the understanding of the pre-schizoid phase itself, and thus *contributes to the understanding of normal development.* For the symptoms of autistic disorder are only partly disease-specific, that is, to be seen in the context of the disavowal of separateness from the object. This includes the symptomatology of imitative fusion, aimed at enforcing the denied fusion through imitation, or the autistic sensation shapes designed to create a non-existent continuous link between the ego and the object. Similarly, the function of the autistic sensation object is to mend the autistic hole.

However, this symptomatology is situated within a symptomatic environment not invented by autists for their symptom formation but encountered as an ambient condition, invaluable to us as it captures, like a time trap, the real presence of qualities I have theoretically inferred from the pre-schizoid phase parameters. For instance, the fixation to a pure, distanceless two-dimensional sensory system unaware of distance modalities. Or residing in a realm of absolute omnipotence, which I deduced theoretically from the lack of object constancy and, consequently, from the absence of any possibility of comparison, regarding both the ego and the object. This is starkly contrasted with actual neoteny at life's outset, in which there is however no capacity of insight. Or the moment of timelessness and spacelessness, which results from the missing object constancy. The perception of time and space is essentially the outcome of an evolving capacity to compare representations, specifically within temporal and spatial dimensions. In essence, the pathology of early childhood autism corroborates that the things that arise as demands from theoretical considerations are actually there. Conversely, our clinical treatment of primary autistic disorders thus has a theory that accurately embeds it metapsychologically.

To summarize, the phenomenology of primary autistic disorder presents a dual aspect: on one side, the foreclosure of the object, along with the ensuing anxieties of being, the diffuse-osmotic anxieties, the autistic sensation object, the autistic sensation shapes, as well as the compensatory imitative phenomena constitute authentic autistic pathology. On the other side, the attachment to the sensorial and tactile, the two-dimensionality, the omnipotence of the ego, and the object as the representation of abundance and completeness are characteristics of the pre-schizoid phase. It is within this phase that primary autism is situated, fixating its conditions and utilizing them in the context of disavowing separateness from the object.

The pre-schizoid phase constitutes an initial form of experience common to all humans, the understanding of which has been unveiled by the pathology of primary autism. We have all traversed a stage where primary omnipotence defines the ego's self-experience, and the object is perceived as the representation of absolute fullness, completeness, and abundance. This amalgamation of the ego's omnipotence and the object's absolute completeness, in a positive scenario, fosters a fundamental – total – affirmation of life, upon which the pre-schizoid phase sustains human existence. Hence, primary autism, with its foreclosure of the object relationship, and the primary affirmation of this relationship, embody the two pivotal themes of the pre-schizoid phase: The utmost negation and the utmost affirmation of the object exist side by side.

The most significant outcome of this study on the metapsychology of psychic origins is that the foundational hypothesis positing the emergence of the psychical from perception can be regarded as validated through the complete concordance of the theoretical deductions from this foundational hypothesis with the phenomenology of primary psychogenic encapsulation autism.

Within the limits of this investigation, the proposition that the psyche arises from perception is thus confirmed.

Essay 3

Three Theses

I

Mark Solms

In my previous work I have demonstrated that mental structure formation and pathogenesis can be deduced from the logical evolution of the perceptual function, that is, from the confrontation between subject and object of perception, which constitutes the act of perception itself. In essence, the phenomenon I have addressed shows that the known stages of structural development emerge step by step as a causal logical derivation from the foundational hypothesis of origin in perception. Through this approach, I aim to have proven that the inception of psychic life is indeed rooted in perception.

As detailed in my research findings, one of the conclusions I've reached is that the concept of the death drive, as Freud described it – namely, as an aggression initially aimed at the self with the goal of dissolving the living structure to return to an inorganic state – does not exist. To revisit, Freud's theoretical mistake lies in his presumption of a necessary change in the object of the death drive, from its original focus on the subject's self to an external object. According to Freud, this prevents the death drive from leading to direct self-destruction.

However, in my perspective, this change of object assumed by Freud is essentially a misperception: it is a change from the inner to the outer object, which latter becomes conceivable for the first time at this point as a consequence of the elaboration of the depressive position. The death drive is directed toward the object before as after. There is no change of the object of the death-drive.

Instead, I understand the death drive as the desire of the primary ego, which has arisen from perception, to fuse with the primary object, which has also arisen from perception, insofar as this object is then the only thing that exists outside of the ego, and therefore, with the occurrence of an unpleasure, must be experienced as the very site of the suspension of this unpleasure. This is, as it were, the primary wish that sets in motion the whole dynamic of psychic structure formation. This fusionary intention becomes – unintentionally – the death drive, since its realization in the abolition of the separation of ego and object would abolish the perceptual function itself – and with it the evolving dimension of the psychical –, insofar as perception arises out of this separation and exists in it. The death drive is therefore the, so to speak, inevitable constructive problem arising from the fact that psychic life has its root in perception.

This desire for fusion can inherently possess a force that supersedes all else, given that no motive within the psyche is stronger than the fundamental need to overcome unpleasure, of unlust. Specifically, the self-interests of the object are utterly irrelevant to the fusion-oriented death drive, whose unconditional pursuit of pleasure may even act against the ego's own self-preservation interests. In this context, we indeed observe the phenomenology of an absolute aggression, which led Freud to postulate a death drive aimed against life itself. However, I view the goal of this aggression not as the creation of a tension-free state in which the living organism disintegrates into its elemental parts, but rather, as I have mentioned, in the unconditional pleasure-seeking of fusion with the object. Such fusion, in phantasy, would eliminate any possibility of unpleasure. To demonstrate the potential pathogenetic power of this process, I point out that it is this fusional impulse that underlies the foreclosure of the withdrawing object – the not-me object – in autistic disorders, thereby engendering autistic pathology.

To elaborate on this point briefly, it is important to be clear that the pressure toward fusion contains the most radical aggression imaginable. In fusion, the intrinsic character of the object is obliterated. Insofar as fusion consists in the fiction of the fusion of ego and object – that is, in the dissolution of the object in the ego – fusionary aggression is narcissistic aggression per se and in pure form. *The fusionary death drive is narcissism.*

In this context, the overall phenomenology associated with the death drive, as originally conceived by Freud, remains unchanged: The fusionary death drive manifests as an unconditional aggression that overrides both the object and the ego. The primary distinction from Freud's interpretation is that I do not view the objective of this death drive as the disintegration of the living into its basic components, as a result of the supposed inevitable labor and thus unpleasure of sustaining a multicellular organism. Instead, I propose that the aim of the death drive is fusion with the object, insofar as the object is perceived by the ego as the locus of suspension of the tension of unpleasure. The underlying principle shared by both perspectives on the death drive is the notion of reducing tension to zero – but precisely not through a biologically driven return to the inorganic state, but through fusion with the object. While practically, the difference between these two theories may seem minimal, theoretically, it represents a significant divergence, which, as I will demonstrate shortly, impacts the entire conceptual framework of the psyche, whether one starts from a death drive founded in the biological.

Given that in this inevitable dynamic of fusion, both ego and object would be annulled, and the dimension of the psychical, which emerges precisely from the juxtaposition and separateness of ego and object, would be undone, I have chosen to retain the term death drive. However, to distinguish from Freud's interpretation, I refer to it as the *psychic* death drive.

In essence, I do not uphold the classical drive theory presented in "Beyond the Pleasure Principle" as valid. Freud's notion of the death drive is notably characterized by its reference to the somatic – specifically, the unpleasure stemming from the labor required to maintain a multicellular organism. In contrast, my interpretation of the death drive is epistemological or logical: perception necessitates the separation and distinctness of ego and object. Psychic structure formation arises from the conflicts to maintain this separation and, based on the morphological conditions of the cortex, leads to reflective consciousness and, consequently, the capacity for abstract thought. As I have demonstrated in the earlier sections of this work, the capacity for abstract thought and reflective consciousness is secured by the Oedipus complex. What is at stake here, then, is cortical functioning, cortical consciousness. The Oedipus complex governs and secures cortical consciousness.

An important theoretical implication arises here. I have shown that the Oedipus complex inevitably arises from the conflicts over securing the separation of ego and object. This results in the ubiquity of the Oedipus complex. Freud, of course, had also perceived this ubiquity, but had concluded from it that there must be phylogenetically transmitted "primary phantasies" (Freud 1915), i.e., phylogenetic memories of concrete events that would be inherited. This was the background and content of his Lamarckism. Solms (2021a) elaborates that such a phylogenetically inherited memory is neuroscientifically impossible, since such a memory, which would revolve, for example, around an experienced castration or the consequence of a transgression of the incest taboo, would be an episodic or semantic memory, i.e., part of declarative memory, which as such is located in the cortex. Cortical memories, however, cannot be inherited. Solms: "(...) the cortex does not contain inherited memories. All innate response patterns are encoded sub-cortically." (2021a p 560)

In contrast to the idea of inherited memory, I propose an alternative explanation for the ubiquity of the Oedipus complex. Its universal presence does not stem from an inherited memory but rather from the inevitable culmination of conflicts over the separation of ego and object into the Oedipus complex, as I have demonstrated. Therefore, the Oedipus complex is not something passed down through generations but rather emerges anew in each individual as a result of psychic structure formation. Freud, while making a correct observation regarding the universal nature of the Oedipus complex, based his conclusion on a flawed explanation, which was also closely tied to his erroneous conception of the death drive.

To underscore, the pivotal assertion concerns the universality of the Oedipus complex. During Freud's era, it was utterly inconceivable to attribute this ubiquity to the unavoidable structural conflicts encountered by every individual possessing a functional psychic apparatus – that is, with normal cortical function and normal perceptual signals. The theoretical framework necessary to support such an explanation had not yet been developed. Thus, Freud's Lamarckism should be seen as a provisional and placeholder theory aimed at accounting for something – the universality of the Oedipus complex – that could not be otherwise explained at the time. Fundamentally, the minutiae of this debate are of lesser importance. The critical breakthrough was the identification of the Oedipus complex and the recognition of its ubiquity. This was Freud's monumental contribution. The discovery of the unconscious, the universal relevance of the Oedipus complex, and the interpretation of dreams compose the radiant triad that has eternally secured Freud's legacy within the annals of human cultural evolution.

In his final, dualistic theory of drives, Freud posited the death drive as stemming from the somatic – specifically, from the unlust associated with the effort, the labor required to maintain a multicellular organism. With the invalidation of this hypothesis, the link to the bodily aspect, so to speak, is left unoccupied, a gap that neuropsychoanalysis claims with a significant degree of scientific legitimacy. Mark Solms, the leading representative in neuropsychoanalysis, demonstrates that the seven "basic emotions" identified by Jaak Panksepp (1998) within his taxonomy of affects not only apply to humans too but constitute comprehensive drive systems that govern human behavior. Solms states, "When it comes to the emotional drives, it turns out that *seven* of them can be reliably elicited by electrical or (specific) chemical stimulation at exactly the same brain sites, in all mammals, from mice to men." (Solms 2021, p 32; emph. MS). Chemically, each of these seven drives correlates with distinct neuromodulators. Furthermore, Solms notes, "all the basic emotional drive circuits (..) are almost entirely subcortical." (op.cit. p 32), highlighting a fundamental subcortical basis for these basic emotional drives.

I list these seven emotional drives, following Panksepp in capital letters: LUST, RAGE, FEAR, PANIC/GRIEF, SEEKING, CARE, PLAY. I will not delve into their specifics and direct those interested to Solms for further details. These drives represent phylogenetically automatized reactions (automated predictions) to standard emotional situations,

126

akin to non-declarative memory, which resides in the subcortical region. Solms explains, "Non-declarative memories are response patterns, as opposed to reminiscences; they can never be brought to mind, they can only be enacted. (...) Non-declarative memories (...) are encoded in subcortical structures" (2021a, p 559), highlighting their role as innate, unconscious, action-oriented memories, distinct from the potentially conscious recollections encoded in cortical structures.

The pathology in this domain essentially stems from the discrepancy between automatized predictions and the demands of current reality. This mismatch gives rise to drive pressure. What is consciously experienced as the drive is this non-correspondence, namely, the error signal. The error signal or drive pressure thus represents that portion of psychic energy not engaged in an effective automatized prediction leading to fulfillment. From an information-theoretical perspective, Karl Friston has termed this discrepancy "free energy." To highlight the innovative nature of this approach, I refer again to Solms: "Drive energy may be equated with Friston free energy and is therefore *quantifiable* in principle" (op.cit. p 54, emph. MS). The fundamental equations pertaining to this concept are detailed in the work of Friston and Solms (2018). This development would indeed satisfy Freud's neuroscientific aspirations.

Before delving into the aspects that are of particular interest to me regarding this framework, I wish to acknowledge the clinical efficacy of this drive model. Clinically, there is no doubt in my mind that these drives exist and profoundly shape and structure both experience and behavior. From my perspective, psychoanalysis has made a substantial advancement by integrating this model, thereby grounding itself in a neuroscientific foundation, as had been Freud's great hope.

The critical inquiry is how the neuroscientific groundworks detailed by Solms intersect with the structural model of the psyche I have presented. I contend that the insights provided by these neuroscientific explorations lead to some profoundly intriguing conclusions about the basic operations and essence of the complex phenomenon that is the human psyche. These insights not only enrich our understanding of psychic dynamics but also bridge historical psychoanalytic concepts with contemporary neuroscientific discoveries.

Addressing the matter from the perspective of the results, I am convinced that Solms' findings indicate the psyche encompasses both subcortical and cortical functional domains. Within the subcortical region, the phylogenetically determined "automatized predictions," as detailed and discussed by Panksepp and Solms, are operational. Undoubtedly, this represents a broad and crucial aspect of experience and behavior, carrying profound implications for psychopathology. I will elaborate on this further in the following sections.

In my own work, I have focused on the cortical area of human mental life, and it is precisely in contrast to Solms' approach that it becomes possible to specify more accurately the core issue: It concerns the phenomenon whereby mental activity is so closely tied to perception – that is, to the dynamics between ego and object – that cortical functioning would be non-existent without perception. Conversely, human perception and its implications for mental structure formation would not be feasible without the cortical morphology.

In practical terms, the essence of this concept is that perception, facilitated by the neuroanatomical configuration of the cortex, generates representations – or in Freud's terminology, "Vorstellungen" – of both the ego and the object. These representations do not merely link to inner experience but also engage in a lawful interaction with one another within a framework defined by logic. Causal logic serves as the operational principle of the cortex. This logical foundation naturally engenders conflicts between the representations from the outset, which, as I have outlined, lead to the entire psychic structure formation as well as to the deviations manifesting in psychopathology that stem from this logical construct.

As I have consistently emphasized, the primary goal of this structure formation is to establish a framework that precludes the danger of fusion between the representations of ego and object. The Oedipus complex plays a pivotal role in achieving this by safeguarding against the potential for these representations to fuse. The inherent structural vulnerability of a system whose primum movens is perception – contingent upon the maintained separation of subject and object of perception – lies in this risk of fusion between ego and object representations.

To quote Solms: "Episodic memories, and semantic ones, are defined by their ideational character (Freud's "Vorstellungen"). That is why they can take the form of thoughts. This characteristic is determined by the fact that they are encoded in cortical tissues, (...). The cerebral cortex literally "maps" inputs from the sensory receptors of the eyes, ears, tongue, skin, muscles, etc." (2021a p 559).

"Vorstellungen," or representations, are indeed tied to the cortex. They are evoked by the "inputs from the sensory receptors", essentially, perceptions.

Given this perspective, the cortex is seen as the site where psychic structural phantasms are constructed from perceptions, forming the basis, and determining the essence of human psychic life. Consequently, for the cortex to undertake this role effectively, it must not be influenced by any pre-existing dispositions or structural preconditions. Solms corroborates this understanding, indicating, "This has led some neuroscientists – such as Panksepp – to the view that cortical tissue is random-access memory space, that is, a blank slate (Panksepp and Biven 2012)" (2021a, p 560f). Additionally, he states, "the newborn neocortex is a tabula rasa" (2021a, p 561), and "the cortical memory systems are essentially blank at birth" (2021a, p 563), underscoring the concept that the cortex is initially unshaped, awaiting the imprint of experiences to form the complex web of human psychical structures.

What does this delineation imply? Clearly, from this point forward, we must differentiate between two domains when considering the psyche: Firstly, the realm of phylogenetic inheritance, encompassed by the emotional drives as outlined by Panksepp and Solms, and secondly, the domain of cortical structure formation and conflict dynamics, epitomized by the oedipal conflict constellation. In stark contrast to the subcortical emotional drives, it becomes evident that the entirety of cortical structure formation is devoted exclusively to the theme of safeguarding the ego against the danger of its dissolution in fusion – that is, protecting it against the psychic death drive. As I have outlined in the previous sections of this book, this process of structural protection of the ego unfolds through various stages, including object splitting, the paranoid-schizoid and depressive positions, the position outside – meaning the position of the ego outside the drive phantasm, connected with the self-reflective split of the ego – and ultimately, the final structural protection of the position outside via the oedipal conflict and its sublimative resolution.

Along this path, the emergence of reflective consciousness, ultimately anchored structurally by the Oedipus complex, takes place in the position outside. From a teleological perspective, one might argue that this emergence serves as the culmination of the entire process. Teleological assumptions do not have a good reputation scientifically. However, it depends on how one defines teleology. In this context, I propose a conceptualization of teleology whereby the morphological-neurological architecture of the cortex – specifically, its commitment to representations – enables, and therefore in fact demands, self-reflective functioning. This conceptualization aligns with the notion of a self-organizing system as defined by W. R. Ashby, suggesting an intrinsic demand for self-aware functioning.

So, the present state of research, as I see it, is that we have to start from two psyches, so to speak: One psyche is that of the emotional drives. We are talking here about phylogenetically automatized reactions (automatized predictions). The pathology in this area is defined by the fact that the automatized prediction does not or not completely correspond to the current reality requirement. What becomes conscious from the drive is this non-correspondence, i.e. the error signal.

The "other" psyche, namely the cortical psyche, is focused on protecting the ego and, by extension, reflective consciousness against the danger of fusion. This domain encompasses the entirety of classical structure formation as I have outlined, including the various forms of psychopathology, which I have identified as manifestations of the ego's evasion in response to the demands for fusional renunciation. It is evident that problems within one domain interlock with those in the other as soon as there is a thematic overlap, or isomorphism, between them. For instance, challenges related to the PANIC/GRIEF drive – or the attachment drive – will inevitably impact fusional dynamics at the cortical domain.

Solms, in his paper "A Revision of Freud's Theory of the Biological Origin of the Oedipus Complex" (2021a), proposes that the Oedipus complex arises from the interplay among the seven emotional drives at the subcortical level, offering a compelling explanation for its emotional dynamics. However, from my perspective, what seems absent is an exploration of the Oedipus complex's deeper dimensions in terms of content that I have delineated: specifically, its significance as a structure that definitively secures the ego against the threat of dissolution through fusion with the object. This critique underscores my view of the relationship between the cortical structural level and the subcortical affective level of the psyche. I believe that the emotional drives not only create an emotional-affective resonance space for the cortical level but are also in a resonant relationship with cortical themes, serving to significantly strengthen and amplify them.

We find ourselves in a situation where Freud's insistence that the drive should be linked to the somatic is entirely satisfied by the emotional drives. This satisfaction at the subcortical level effectively exempts the cortical realm from this requirement. Freud had not anticipated the possibility of essentially two distinct psyches. From my perspective, it appears that the conflict-driven structural dynamics at the cortical level adhere strictly to the principle of causal logic, grounded in representations ("Vorstellungen") derived from perception. Conversely, as Solms articulates, the cortex operates as a tabula rasa, devoid of any intrinsic forces, in stark contrast to the subcortical area, which is dominated by the innate response patterns of emotional drives.

To clarify the essential critique, Solms has illustrated that the death drive, as Freud conceptualized it, does not exist as a biological imperative within subcortical functions. However, this revelation does not address the role or existence of the death drive at the cortical level. My research indicates that the process of structure formation at the cortical level inevitably gives rise to two diametrically opposed psychic forces. One of these forces, if left unchecked, would lead to the dissolution of the psychic dimension itself, thereby justifying its identification as the psychic death drive. Consequently, Freud's conceptualization of dual drives is accurate at the cortical level, with the caveat that the death drive does not originate from organic or biological roots as he initially proposed.

The research of Panksepp and Solms regarding emotional drives has demonstrated that Freud's concept of a death drive rooted in the soma lacks neuroscientific support. My own arguments have also contested Freud's biological basis for the death drive, but the critique gains a more definitive edge when bolstered by neuroscientific evidence. This revelation doesn't so much introduce a new scenario as it uncovers the true nature of an existing one: It becomes evident that the cortical psyche – encompassing all that I've described in terms of psychic structure formation and the resulting psychopathology – operates autonomously. It derives its substantial energetic force from within itself, without specific replenishment or support from the somatic realm.

At first glance, the autonomy of the cortical psyche may not seem particularly groundbreaking, but a deeper analysis unveils its radical implications: For instance, where does the energy come from that transforms the fusionary realization – the merging of ego and object representations – into the quintessential event of fear? What is the source of the catastrophic impact that causes the foreclosure of the object in cases of encapsulated primary autism to result in a total halt of further development? How do we explain all the other pathological phenomena and their consequences? How is it that the resolution of the conflict of the infantile depressive position is contingent upon the ego's position outside the drive phantasm, that is, the position outside?

From my observation and understanding, the response to these queries unfolds in two parts: Firstly, the cortical psyche is composed entirely of representations – those inner depictions of a subject's external and internal experiences that Freud termed "Vorstellungen." Secondly, the interrelations among these representations are governed solely by the principle of causal logic. This implies, for instance, that the destructive impact of fusing the representations of the ego and the primary object is driven exclusively by causal logic, namely, the necessity of keeping ego and object separate for perception to function. Therefore, the reality principle – the straightforward fact that specific causes lead to specific consequences – prevails as the dominant force in the cortical realm. Put simply, the foundational principle is truth. As long as the organism lives, these processes are energetically sustained by the very fact of life, whereby every effect transitions into the cause of a subsequent outcome, epitomizing the flow of time.

The distinctive phenomenon that characterizes and defines the human species is that the sequences of cause and effect, operating on the morphological foundation of the cortex, invariably result in reflective consciousness, provided there are no pathological deviations, which themselves follow a distinct logic. This encompasses the overarching significance of my exposition. The cortical psyche constitutes the realm of psychoanalysis. Even the emotional drives identified by Panksepp and Solms need to be translated into the language of the cortical psyche, meaning into representations, for them to be psychically processed.

II

The Object as Representation of the Life Drive

The second, fundamental consideration that holds importance for me in these concluding remarks logically extends from the prior discussion but addresses an entirely distinct domain: In the therapeutic context of patients emerging from primary encapsulated autism, we are met with the exceptionally challenging and strenuous task of forming an object relation and, indeed, an object representation for these patients. For those more closely involved in these matters, I am referring to such issues as the anxieties of being, the osmotic-diffuse anxieties, adhesive identifications/equations, mantling phenomena, the object-implant and the complexities involved in establishing a bisexual container. Given that primary autistic pathology stems from a primary foreclosure of object representation, it seems logical to interpret all these challenges in reversing this foreclosure as a laborious reconstructive catching up of processes that occur spontaneously and swiftly in the course of normal development.

Admittedly, we are navigating through highly speculative territory. Building upon the previous discussions regarding the genesis of the (cortically) psychical from perception, I wish to propose a potentially significant notion: If perception involves the spontaneous emergence of the ego and the representation of the primary object, and if the psychic death drive is expressed through the ego's fusional movement towards the primary object – a movement that would annul both the ego and the object, thereby collapsing the newly emerged dimension of the psychical – then the representation of the object unaffected by fusion and protected against fusion has to be seen as the manifestation of the life drive within the psyche.

As I have demonstrated, the entire course of psychic structural development, reaching its pinnacle in the Oedipus complex, is aimed at establishing such a structural protection of the object imago from the fusional assault. Thus, I propose the idea that the primordial representation of the primary object is imbued with its complete potential force of cathexis from the moment it first emerges in the initial act of perception, possessing its full synthetic importance as the bearer of the life drive. I argue that it is this object imago, free from the threat of fusion, that crucially propels the development of the psychic structure from the very beginning.

In essence, I aim to convey that the primordial object representation, which emerges spontaneously in the first act of perception, represents *the* paramount psychic protective imago, embodying the core manifestation of the life drive. Ideally, under its protection, psychic development proceeds entirely unaffected by the psychic abysses encountered, for example, in the treatment of primary autistic patients. These abysses signify the disintegration of the object imago as it veers towards a death-drive induced, fusionary realization – essentially, the disintegration of the psychical itself. The autonomous object imago, unchallenged by fusion, represents the psyche's safeguard against the sole internal threat it faces: the death drive. This autonomous object imago is ultimately structurally laid down in the sublimative ego ideal, as the resolution of the oedipal conflict. Thus, the ego ideal, as I have detailed in the previous sections of this book, serves as the instance of structurally securing the separation of ego and object and thus the instance of securing the psychical.

Indeed, I acknowledge that in proposing this concept, I am delineating an ideal. However, I prefer to term it not as an ideal but as a principle that is actualized to varying degrees, influenced by the prevailing external and internal, constitutional circumstances, and the associated initial conditions for the death drive. In this sense, the primordial imago of the primary object, as the manifestation of the life drive, metaphorically resembles Athena emerging fully armored from the head of Zeus – a symbol of innate wisdom and protection springing forth, fully formed and ready.

I surmise, therefore, that the challenges we encounter in trying to reestablish object relations in patients emerging from primary

136

autism are not solely due to the necessity of artificially reigniting a developmental process that faltered in its natural progression. We are also contending with individuals who remain subject to the sway of an excessively potent death drive. From this perspective, the treatment of autistic patients indeed represents a Sisyphean task – an endeavor of continuous effort and persistence, akin to the mythological punishment of Sisyphos, doomed to eternally roll a boulder up a hill only for it to roll down again each time it nears the summit. In any case, this is the danger.

III

Anorexia and Bulimia as Autistic Breakdown

The discussion on Frances Tustin's discoveries regarding the psychodynamics of psychogenic primary encapsulated autism significantly influenced the development of my theoretical framework. Her descriptions of the fusional assault on the object, the subsequent emergence of the rejecting not-me object, and the ensuing reactive foreclosure of this object provided crucial clinical evidence for my considerations. This evidence was drawn from what is arguably the earliest and most severe form of mental illness.

Over the years, the study of autistic disorders and phenomena has seen a substantial global increase. Through this expanded research, it has become evident that Frances Tustin's contributions extend well beyond her specialization in a particularly severe form of early childhood mental illness. In my view, her pivotal discovery is the psychological possibility of completely foreclosing the relationship to the object and the dire consequences of such foreclosure. This insight places her among the ranks of psychoanalysis's other great pioneers: Freud, who unveiled the unconscious and the Oedipus complex; Melanie Klein, identified for her discovery of the object's early good-bad split; and Tustin herself, who elucidated the pathology associated with the withdrawal of cathexis from the object.

The recognition of the broad significance of this discovery is gradually becoming more widespread, as mentioned earlier, thereby enhancing the understanding of the role of autistic phenomena across a variety of clinical conditions – or, more precisely, the significance of the withdrawal of cathexis, the foreclosure of the object in diverse clinical contexts. In this vein, I wish to use these concluding remarks to highlight to my colleagues that, in my perspective, anorexia and bulimia represent fully manifested autistic clinical conditions. This line of reasoning originates from a statement by Joshua Durban, which encapsulates the Kleinian psychodynamic perspective on anorexia: "We starve the object inside, the object inside is starving us, and we need to starve both ourselves and the object as a service to the death drive. This constitutes a lock-in: we can't get in." To this, he added the anorectic individual's relationship with greed (personal communication, 2023).

Rephrased slightly, we arrive at a concise definition of autism according to Tustin's perspective: The internal object that starves us represents the evading not-me object; the object that we internally starve is the autistic foreclosure of this evading not-me object; and greed manifests as the overarching fusional intent driving the entire process.

In essence, the psychodynamics of anorexia are distinctly autistic. Given the prevalence of anorexia – millions of people affected globally, with a significant number facing mortality – it cannot simply be regarded as a mere autistic enclave or pocket. I suggest we view it as a full autistic breakdown, akin to a schizophrenic breakdown occurring during puberty or adolescence. This argument could be broadened to include bulimia in parallel as the breakdown equivalent of what Frances Tustin termed primary confusional autism, which exhibits a slightly more object-oriented approach than primary encapsulated autism, the latter being more closely aligned with anorexia proper in this analogy.

To clarify my stance, I am convinced that anorexia and bulimia represent the specific and exclusive forms of autistic breakdown when it manifests – so to speak, belatedly – within the context of a developed personality organization. Under such conditions, an autistic collapse takes the form of either anorexia or bulimia. The significant sensory dependence observed in eating disorders further indicates an autistic trajectory. Moreover, the fundamental forces that facilitate the diagnosis of an autistic condition, including movement, connectivity, receptivity, reciprocity, and splitting, are markedly impaired or disrupted, thus undeniably pointing towards a clear autistic nature.

From this discussion, three main consequences emerge:

The first is epidemiological, highlighting that two of the most prevalent functional-psychosomatic conditions are causally autistic.

The second consequence holds the greatest significance from a scientific perspective. It asserts that an autistic disorder, in the most direct and complete sense, can manifest within the framework of an otherwise developed personality organization. This is not, as mentioned, about secondary forms of manifestation akin to an autistic pocket or enclave.

The third implication pertains to treatment techniques: If anorexia and bulimia are indeed autistic disorders in the fullest sense, then all our insights regarding treatment methods for autistic conditions must be applied to these disorders. Any other approach is unlikely to be effective.

This necessitates a shift in our thinking, as we are traditionally used to associating primary autistic disorder with severely affected children who are unable to communicate or speak. Frances Tustin attributed the severity of this clinical picture to the fact that these children have foreclosed the object relationship at such an early stage, thereby obstructing all further psychological development.

Anorexia and bulimia present us with the reality that such a foreclosure of the object relationship can also take place at a later stage of personality development. Therefore, this foreclosure, that is, the withdrawal of cathexis from the object, is identified as the core autistic process and, consequently, as Frances Tustin's true discovery.

Bibliography

Bick E (1968). The experience of the skin in early object relations. Int J Psychoanal 49:484–6.

Bick E (1986). Further considerations on the function of the skin in early object relations. Br J Psychother 2:292–9.

Bion W R (1962a). The psycho-analytic study of thinking. *Int. J. Psycho-Anal. 43. 306-310.*

Bion W R (1962b). *Learning from Experience.* London : Heinemann.

Bion W R (1970). Attention and Interpretation. London: Heinemann.

Chasseguet-Smirgel J (1975). L'Idéal du Moi. Essai psychanalytique sur la 'maladie d'Idéalité'. Paris: Tchou.

Chasseguet-Smirgel J (2003). The question of the father. In: The Body as Mirror of the World (2005, 26-41), Free Association Books: London.

Durban J (2014). Despair and hope: on some varieties of countertransference and enactment in the psychoanalysis of ASD (autistic spectrum disorder) children. *J of Child Psychotherapy, Vol. 40, Issue 2*, pp. 187–200.

Durban J (2017). In the beginning was the Word? The changing shape and use of interpretations in the analyses of ASD and psychotic children (unpublished manuscript).

Durban J (2021). Where does the Covid live? Osmotic/diffuse anxieties, isolation, and containment in times of the plague. In: Howard B. Levine & Ana de Staal (Eds) Psychoanalysis and

Covidian Life: Common Distress, Individual Experience. London: Phoenix Books.

Freud S (1915). A Case of Paranoia Running Counter to the Psycho-Analytic Theory. S.E., 10: 242.

Freud S (1917). Mourning and Melancholia. S. E., 14: 243–258.

Freud S (1924). The Economic Problem of Masochism. S. E., 19: 159–172.

Freud S (1927). Fetishism. S.E., 21: pp. 152–158.

Freud S (1933). New Introductory Lectures on Psycho-Analysis. S.E., 22:1–182.

Freud S (1938). An Outline of Psycho-Analysis. S. E., 23: 144--08.

Haag G (1985). La mère et le bébé dans les deux moitiés du corps. Neuropsychiatrie de l'Enfance 33:107–14.

Haag G, Tordjman S, Duprat A, Urwand S, Jardin F, Clement MC, Cukierman A, Druon C, Maufras du Chatellier A, Tricaud J, Dumont A-M (2005). Psychodynamic assessment of changes in children with autism under psychoanalytic treatment. Int J Psychoanal 86:335–52.

Klein M (1957). Envy and Gratitude. The Writings of Melanie Klein (Vol. 3), 176-235. London: Hogarth, 1975.

Maiello S (1997). Going beyond: notes on the beginning of object relations in light of "The perpetuation of an error". In: Encounters with Autistic States. Northvale, NJ: Jason Aronson.

McDougall J (1972). Primal scene and sexual perversion. Int J Psychoanal 53: pp. 371–384.

McDougall J (1978). Plaidoyer pour une certaine anormalité. Paris: Gallimard.

Panksepp J & Biven L (2012). Archaeology of Mind. New York: Norton.

Rhode M (2012). Whose memories are they and where do they go? Problems surrounding internalization in children on the autistic spectrum. Int J Psychoanal (2012) 93:355–376.

Rosenfeld H (1964). On the psychopathology of narcissism: a clinical approach. Int J Psychoanal 45: pp. 332–337.

Segal H (1957). Notes on symbol formation. Int J Psychoanal 8:391/7. Republished (1981) in The Work of Hanna Segal. New York: Jason Aronson, pp.49–65.

Segal H (1978). On symbolism. *Int J Psychoanal 59:* 315–19.

Solms M & Friston K (2018). How and why consciousness arises: Some considerations from physics and physiology. Journal of Consciousness Studies 25:202–238.

Solms Mark (2021a). A Revision of Freud's Theory of the Biological Origin of the Oedipus Complex. The Psychoanalytic Quarterly, 2021 Volume XC, Number 4.

Solms Mark (2021b). Revision of Drive Theory. JAPA XX/X.

Steiner J (1993). Psychic Retreats. Pathological Organizations in Psychotic, Neurotic and Borderline Patients. London/New York: Routledge.

Tustin F (1972). Autism and Childhood Psychosis. London: Hogarth,New York: Jason Aronson.

Tustin F (1981). Autistic States in Children. London/New York: Routledge.

Tustin F (1986). Autistic Barriers in Neurotic Patients. London: Karnac Books.

Tustin F (1988). Psychotherapy with Children who Cannot Play. Int. Rev. Psycho-Anal., (15):93–106.

Tustin F (1994a). Autistic Barriers in Neurotic Patients, 2nd edn. London: Karnac.

Tustin F (1994b). The perpetuation of an error. Journal of Child Psychotherapy 20:3–23.

Winnicott DW (1949). Birth memories, birth trauma, and anxiety. In: Through paediatrics to psychoanalysis, 174–93. London: Tavistock, 1958. [(1975). London: Hogarth.

Zagermann P (2019). Psychoanalysis: A General Theory of Psychical Structure Formation and Pathogenesis. New York: Analytic Press.

Zagermann P (2019) Psychoanalyse: Eine allgemeine Theorie der psychischen Strukturbildung und Pathogenese. New York: Analytic Press/Kindle e-book.

Zagermann P (2021). Grundzüge einer allgemeinen Theorie der Psychoanalyse Teil I, Omnipotenz und Todestrieb. *Tagungsband der Herbsttagung 2021 der Deutschen Psychoanalytischen Vereinigung (DPV).*

Zagermann P (2022). Grundzüge einer allgemeinen Theorie der Psychoanalyse Teil II, Ichideal und annihilatorische Aggression. *Tagungsband der Herbsttagung 2022 der Deutschen Psychoanalytischen Vereinigung (DPV).*

www.ingramcontent.com/pod-product-compliance
Lightning Source LLC
Chambersburg PA
CBHW060234030426

42335CB00014B/1452